"Wouldn't it be great if every Christian got it that serving others is normal, and if every church became the greatest servant organization in its community? This is exactly the wake-up call needed for those of us drifting off to sleep from the pseudosoothing strains of the 'serve me first' messages that surround us. It's a new day, and *The Outward-Focused Life* may well revolutionize the way we do church—and life."

—**Bill Hybels**, senior pastor, Willow Creek Community Church

"Do I like this book? My first case is on order from the publisher! A story is the quickest point between two hearts, and this is the ultimate story-book about serving. Dave Workman has hit the nail on the head. Serving, generosity, and respect are not aspects of a left-brained program—they are all part of the 'new normal' of God's presence in us that overflows to others. The big things in life are caught—and then clarified with words. So it is with serving. Dave shows this to us with Velcro-like stories.

"If you hope to draw others into a lifestyle of serving, reading this book is a no-brainer. Buy multiples of this book; give, loan, cajole— sometimes life comes down to a whatever-it-takes policy. This is one of those times. The message is just that important and life changing."

—**Steve Sjogren**, author, *Conspiracy of Kindness*

"The last time I saw Dave, he was skateboarding over to the children's church to show them how fun, how relevant, and how balanced a Christian can really be. Loving and serving others with no strings attached was truly the way that Jesus fished. Follow Dave's advice—if you can catch him!"

—**Laurie Beth Jones**, author, *Jesus, CEO*; *The Path*; and *Jesus, Life Coach*

"A successful pastor's urgent call for servanthood. Few things would be more powerful than the realization of Workman's prediction that servanthood will soon become the defining characteristic of Christians. These short, lively pieces—packed full of fascinating stories—show you how to serve."

—**Ronald J. Sider**, author, *The Scandal of Evangelical Politics*; president, Evangelicals for Social Action

"Today the best explanation of the Good News of Jesus is a people who live as he did—as a servant. Dave Workman, through amazing, imagination-shaping stores, shows us all how to participate in an others-focused, outward life."

—**Todd Hunter**, president, Alpha USA

"Dave Workman says, 'There's something new sneaking into the church.' He says there's 'a slow evolution' going on. And it's something good: the rediscovery of loving servanthood as the mark of the Christian. Dave dreams of a time when Christians aren't known for their politics or arguments or scandals, but for the way they love and serve and seek the common good. If enough of us take to heart his message about servanthood and the outward-focused life, we could help make that dream come true."

—**Brian McLaren**, author, speaker, activist (brianmclaren.net)

"Dave Workman is a cultural architect of the church, second to none. He knows the power of stories to move the Jesus community toward embodying her founder's love for a new generation. And he has a genius for going into his city in creative ways to craft the stories he tells. Read, be inspired, and go make your own stories!"

—**Ken Wilson**, senior pastor, Vineyard Church of Ann Arbor;
author, *Jesus Brand Spirituality*

"A major mark of the church in the New Testament was that it existed not for itself but for Christ and the world. The early church loved others through action and started a revolution that changed the world for Christ. The Vineyard Church of Cincinnati is one of those rare, innovative churches that is continuing the revolution in our day. In my friend Dave Workman's new book, which is filled with great stories from his church's own experience, you will catch a glimpse of the profoundly simple strategy that 'small things done with great love will change the world.'

"What I love most about Dave is his passion for sharing God's love in practical ways outside the four walls of a church building. If you are interested in doing more than just speaking to other Christians, you need to read this book!"

—**Rich Nathan**, senior pastor, Vineyard Church of Columbus

The Outward-Focused Life

*Becoming a Servant
in a Serve-Me World*

Dave Workman

BakerBooks
a division of Baker Publishing Group
Grand Rapids, Michigan

Published by Baker Books
a division of Baker Publishing Group
P.O. Box 6287, Grand Rapids, MI 49516-6287
www.bakerbooks.com

Printed in the United States of America

Library of Congress Cataloging-in-Publication Data
Workman, Dave, 1953–
    The outward-focused life : becoming a servant in a serve-me world / Dave Workman.
      p. cm.
    ISBN 978-0-8010-7150-8 (pbk.)
    1. Christian life. 2. Service (Theology). I. Title.
  BV4520.W64 2008
  248.4—dc22   2008008525

For Anita. My love always.
And Rachel and Katie.

Contents

Acknowledgments 9

Introduction 11

Collection One: On Being a Servant 15

Collection Two: Availability 47

Collection Three: Generosity 67

Collection Four: Attitude 85

Collection Five: Grace 103

Collection Six: The Ultimate Servant 125

Collection Seven: The Community of Servants 133

Collection Eight: Small Things 157

Collection Nine: The Effects of Serving on the Servant 173

Conclusion 185

Notes 187

Acknowledgments

Thanks to the following: Vineyard Community Church in Cincinnati—you rock; Jim Smith, who got this project rolling; Donna Hern for everything; Kande Wilson and the outreach team and Claudia Hrinda, who helped write and shape these thoughts; Rob Reider, compadre and engineer; Garry Shirk and the hardest-working church staff who make visionary ministry not just manageable but fun; Jim and Dana Cochran ("In the beginning . . ."); Glenn Drees and Ron Heineman for encouragement over the years; everyone who ever jumped in with us and washed a car, handed out water, wrapped a gift, gave a newspaper away, or cleaned a toilet in the name of Jesus; the Hyrnes for a refuge to write; the Gang With No Name that meets in our living room every second and fourth Wednesday; Andy and Kate White, Jason and Michelle Scott, and Martin Bühlmann for spreading the luv; Chad Allen, my editor Jessica Miles, and the crew at Baker; Clyde Miller, who introduced me to the Servant; and, of course, my friend Steve Sjogren. Special thanks to Mom, who walks out faithfulness every day.

Introduction

For even the Son of Man did not come to be served, but to serve, and to give his life as a ransom for many.

Mark 10:45

American Christians are very similar to American non-Christians in one striking way: most of us want to know what the Next Big Thing is. Very few want to miss the "cutting edge." Whether it's a wave of evangelism; community; organic or methodical church growth; bohemian, green-focused, emerging, or ancient-future paradigms; or whatever—we want to ride it. And rightfully so. None of us wants to be irrelevant and voiceless when we have the ultimate message. We at least want to be catching the wake of the tipping point. Because our culture is drenched in a youth orientation, we have a fear of being outdated, as in "that was so fifteen minutes ago." College alternative-music radio was the king of Right Now, but more high school–produced radio programs are popping up. Look out. And everyone is aware of how MySpace is changing the way music is listened to, especially when television producers hire music scouts to scan the millions of MySpace music pages, looking for unsigned (and cheap) or indie artists to do background scores for their hip new show attempting to capture that coveted demographic: eighteen- to twenty-five-year-olds.

All that to say, I'd like to make a prophetic stab at what the Next Big Thing is.

A few days ago I was visiting a church about a thousand miles from where I pastor. It was good to be anonymous and—pastoral confession here—not be analytical, critical, or concerned about the presentation. About four hundred people were present, and the church was a tribe unconnected with mine, one known more for tradition. I wasn't expecting the worship time to be anything similar to our church's particular style, but interestingly enough, it consisted of the pop band format. I smiled, thinking how that format would have been unheard of in this particular denomination not too many years ago. The worship music wars have mostly died down now. Drums are hardly daring, let alone guitars. Even in traditional settings, you can spot people with their eyes closed and their hands in front of them, palms up. Radical—a few decades ago. Evolution wins over revolution . . . and here we are. Contemporary worship is no longer daring. It's accepted, not even reluctantly. Even the charismatic versus cessationist arguments that were sometimes connected to style have mostly lumbered off like dinosaurs.

There's something new sneaking into the church, and in a few decades, it will be pervasive.

Here's my Next Big Thing prediction: churches in America will become known less for their styles, for their tribes, for their proselytizing methods, for their politics, for their clamoring over Christian "rights," for the things they're against . . . and more for the way they serve. Servanthood will be the defining characteristic of people who are followers of Jesus.

The question I regularly ask myself as a pastor in Cincinnati is this: what if the "Big C" Church in our city was known more for serving than for any other thing?

The Roman Empire was once ruled by an emperor known as Julian the Apostate, a title given him because he abandoned Christianity (which had been forced upon him) and then went on a massive campaign to restore pagan worship, even publicly performing sacrifices of bulls to the pagan gods. He hated Christians and once wrote an angry letter regarding, of all things, the effectiveness of Christianity: "These impious Galileans not only feed their own poor, but ours also; welcoming them into their agapae [love feasts], they attract them, as children are attracted, with cakes. Whilst the pagan priests neglect the poor, the hated Galileans devote themselves to works of charity."[1]

I predict a slow evolution of churches being characterized by servanthood as the norm rather than anything stylistic, political, or even theological. Not that those things are unimportant, but the face of the Western church must change in light of virtually no real persecution. Change or persecution must happen for survival.

It was during one of these thought processes that I was presented with the idea of doing a daily two-minute radio program on a local Christian station. At first I was uninterested; I simply happen not to be a Christian radio listener. And then it dawned on me: *Hey, pea brain, you've got a built-in audience of churchgoers. What if they really became servants of lost people? It could change the spiritual climate of a city. Or at least how people perceive the church.*

And so what follows is a collection of some of the hundreds of radio spots that were produced. They are roughly categorized, although each vignette is meant to be thought provoking on its own.

But I'll let you decide that.

Collection One

On Being a Servant

Sometime back I walked into a fast-food place that was freezing. People were eating with their coats on. I was waiting on my food and said to the woman at the cash register, "Hey, it's pretty chilly in here."

She smiled and said, "Yeah, that's how we like it back here. It gets warm in the kitchen."

I replied, "Yeah, but the people sitting out here are eating with their coats on."

She looked at the dining area and then back at me like I was from another planet and said, "I know. But this is how we like it back here."

Being the astute observer of humankind that I am, I knew this wasn't going anywhere. I ate my cheeseburger with my coat on.

That's a picture of many of our churches. We like it a certain way "back here," and the people who can't relate to the language, style, customs, and music are sitting in our churches with their emotional coats on, freezing to death. We frankly don't care about them. We like it like this. We're comfortable, and this is how we've always done it. A few decades ago we would have used this argument regarding traditional versus contemporary, hymns versus choruses, or pipe organs versus drums. But I would rather turn this argument into a philosophical case for inwardness versus outwardness—and what I just described is the total opposite of an outward focus.

If we see others sitting with their coats on and can only say, "That's the way we like it back here," eventually there won't be anyone left in the church except for a few people who think that it's normal to be miserable there. And eventually they'll get to the place where they think that since they're miserable, everyone else should be too.

It was Jesus himself who said in Mark 10:45, "The Son of Man did not come to be served, but to serve, and to give his life as a ransom for many." I wonder what would happen if we saw the church's primary duty as serving lost people.

It could start a movement.

I received an email that began, "I belong to Cobblestone Community Church in Oxford, Ohio, and our mission is 'to love people into life-changing encounters with God.' To do this, we try to reach skeptics and seekers, to lead them to be saved by Christ and teach them to serve. [In other words,] from skeptic to seeker to saved to servant."

I like that continuum. I think most of us who are interested in spiritual development tend to see people move from "seeker" to something we might call "disciple." But what if the end result was actually "servant"? What a statement that would make—and maybe "servant" is more theologically correct.

Think about these verses of Philippians 2, and keep in mind that Paul wrote this letter while in jail: "Your attitude should be the same that Christ Jesus had. Though he was God, he did not demand and cling to his rights as God. He made himself nothing; he took the humble position of a slave and appeared in human form. And in human form he obediently humbled himself even further by dying a criminal's death on a cross" (Phil. 2:5–8 NLT).

Something happens to us when we quit clamoring for our rights and submit to God's sovereign work in our lives. We become less interested in being right or having power or control; instead we understand that being a servant means relinquishing what we want for the greater good of God's desires. Jesus—who created the world and holds the universe together—let go of all power to become a servant of the human race in order to set us free. The Christmas story is the ultimate tale of the prince and the pauper. The incarnation is simply God slipping into human skin in order to rescue us. He made himself nothing, and we're encouraged to have that same attitude, to practice incarnational Christianity and slip into a servant's disguise.

When we get right down to it, it's embarrassing to talk about "our sacrifices for God" in light of the one who gave his life for us ungrateful, self-centered knuckleheads. The writer of Hebrews describes it like this: "Remember those earlier days after you had received the light, when you stood your ground in a great contest in the face of suffering. Sometimes you were publicly exposed to insult and persecution; at other times you stood side by side with those who were so treated. You sympathized with those in prison and joyfully accepted the confiscation of your property, because you knew that you yourselves had better and lasting possessions" (Heb. 10:32–34).

Let's get real: not many of us in the Western world have had our property wrenched away because we follow Jesus. Then again, later the author of Hebrews reminds his audience, "In your struggle against sin, you have not yet resisted to the point of shedding your blood" (Heb. 12:4).

What are my real sacrifices in the journey toward becoming a servant?

I've noticed that Christians who have developed an outward-focused approach to life believe they have a heavenly Father who liberally loves them. That belief is an act of faith. I've sat with believers who have told me, "I just can't believe that God really loves me." There are times when I've said to them, "Wow, that's too bad . . . because it's not true. But if you want to believe a lie about God, that's up to you." This matter is simply about choosing to believe and act on God's Word. You can choose to believe the one who gave his Son as the ultimate expression of his love, or you can choose not to. But real faith is active; it's not sitting around hoping something is true.

I love the Message translation of Luke 12:29–32. Jesus said,

> What I'm trying to do here is get you to relax, not be so preoccupied with getting so you can respond to God's giving. People who don't know God and the way he works fuss over these things, but you know both God and how he works. Steep yourself in God-reality, God-initiative, God-provisions. You'll find all your everyday human concerns will be met. Don't be afraid of missing out. You're my dearest friends! The Father wants to give you the very kingdom itself.

You can either choose to believe that and get a whole new worldview, or you can debate until you're blue in the face. You choose what your truth source is going to be, and ultimately, every truth source will be outside of yourself.

French philosopher, mathematician, and all-around genius Blaise Pascal had an accident that changed the course of his life when he was thirty-one years old. He was nearly killed when horses pulling his carriage bolted on a bridge and left him dangling over the river Seine. He said he had a vision of God while unconscious and later wrote the vision down on paper, which he kept in the lining of his coat the rest of his life. He wrote, "The year of grace 1654. Monday November 23rd . . . certainty, certainty . . . joy, peace . . . God of Jesus Christ. . . . Joy, joy, joy, tears of joy.

. . . May I never be separated from him. . . . Reconciliation sweet and complete." He was forever changed and died only eight years later. You have to love the logic of someone who would later write, "It is not certain that everything is uncertain."[1]

When I first became a Christian, I worked with a man who liked to argue with me about the authenticity and credibility of Christianity. His point was that no one could really know; no one could be certain of the truth. He was into the writings of a philosopher named Krishnamurti.

Krishnamurti was an interesting guy. In the early 1900s, when he was only fourteen years old, he was adopted by a group of people called the Theosophical Society. They believed he was the coming world teacher who would be the reincarnation of Christ in the West and Buddha in the East. He was groomed as the next messiah. At one point they believed he would visit Australia by walking on water. (He took a boat instead.) But in his midthirties, Krishnamurti renounced everything, saw it all as a sham, disbanded the group who believed he was the messiah, and left. He later wrote, "Truth is a pathless land, and you cannot approach it by any path whatsoever."[2] In essence, all you can really trust is yourself; no authority can come from the outside.

One day my co-worker said to me, "Krishnamurti basically says you cannot trust anyone as a source of spiritual knowledge and authority except for your own self and your own senses."

I replied, "So why should I believe him?"

God is deeply in love with you. That's a truth that comes from outside you.

Learning to serve others comes easily from a confidence in knowing who we are. There are really only three big questions in life: Where did I come from? Where am I going? Why am I here? When those three questions are answered, you are free to be anything, with no need to prove something to yourself or anyone else.

It is one thing to think of Jesus as the Son of Man, but it is something far different to see him as the Son of God, God himself in the flesh. When Jesus washed the feet of his disciples, Judas was there. He had not yet run out of the room at their last Passover meal. Jesus washed the feet of the one who would soon betray him. He served the traitor. But what is telling is the confidence Jesus had in who he himself was. And John records in John 13 that Jesus had answered those three big philosophical questions: "Jesus knew that the Father had put all things under his power, and that he had come from God and was returning to God; so he got up from the meal, took off his outer clothing, and wrapped a towel around his waist. After that, he poured water into a basin and began to wash his disciples' feet, drying them with the towel that was wrapped around him" (vv. 3–5).

Jesus knew where he had come from, where he was going, and why he was here. When you know that, you're free to be anything, to take on the lowliest job without concern. If you're a follower of Jesus, you know that you had no hope of saving yourself from yourself and that you can now walk boldly before the throne of grace, simply because of what Jesus did on your behalf. And you know what you're here for: to bring lost children home to their Father. You can live with zero identity crises. As a follower of Jesus, you should be among the freest people on the planet, utterly confident in your Father's love, knowing where you came from and that you will be forever in his presence.

That makes you free to serve in the lowliest, smallest way, knowing you are already a child of a great king. It's easy to clean a toilet for free for a local business knowing that you don't have to prove to anyone who you really are. There's no more posing: you've got nothing to prove because you've already gained it all.

Have you ever written a word on paper, and the more you looked at it, the stranger it looked, like some foreign term that didn't mean anything to you?

Sometimes I think the word *love* is like that. Maybe it's become an alien word in our culture. We love our friends. We love a particular movie. We love our ferret. We love caramel mocha frappuccinos. We love our car.

Something's not right.

The Greeks had several different words that we translate as "love." Each one had a different emotional hook, a different emphasis. The city of Philadelphia comes from one of those Greek words, *phileo*, meaning brotherly love. Our word *erotic* comes from the Greek word *eros*, usually defining a more passionate or sexual love. Christians sometimes use the word *agape*, describing a more deliberate, self-forgetting love.

When we speak of the love God has for us or his commandment that we love one another, we might forget that love is a verb; there is action connected with it. No action, no real love. And so it makes me wonder: if the word *love* has become so misused and abused, what if we exchanged it with the word *serve* instead?

I posed that question one time at our church, and a few weeks later I got an interesting response from someone who told me he began thinking about his wife that way. What if, instead of saying he loved her, he began saying he served her? He began thinking about ways he could creatively serve her. That's love in action. Maybe that's why Paul wrote in Ephesians 6:7, "Serve wholeheartedly, as if you were serving the Lord, not men."

Try it for a week: substitute the word *serve* for *love*, and see what happens. I bet you'll no longer say, "I serve my car" without thinking, *Ouch. I wonder if I really do.*

S ometimes people ask me, "Dave, with all this outward-focused talk, don't you ever think we should be introspective?" Absolutely. Human beings are a complicated mix of history and DNA, complex mechanisms created by nature and nurture. Every so often I'll shock myself by saying something that sounds just like my dad, who's been dead for over twenty-five years. How we determine our worth, how we treat others, how we keep our secrets, how we hide our shame—all are in the mix of who we believe we are. And into that tangled jungle of fear and pride, bluster and brokenness, Jesus wants to lead a discovery expedition—to clean out the brush, to create new paths, to find the passageway to God's heart through the mountains in our psyches.

Solomon said it like this: "The LORD's searchlight penetrates the human spirit, exposing every hidden motive" (Prov. 20:27 NLT). In the healing process of my soul, *why* I do something is more important than *what* I do. When we allow God access to the deepest areas of our lives, true change begins to happen. As the Lord explores each new area, he asks, "May I come in here?" And the reason he asks is because true soul healing is collaborative. That's why David prayed, "Investigate my life, O God, find out everything about me; cross-examine and test me, get a clear picture of what I'm about" (Ps. 139:23 Message).

Sometimes we talk about inviting Jesus into our heart and then, as part of the healing process, inviting him into each room of our heart's "house." But let me challenge you. You can tell when you're becoming more mature in the faith when you say, "Wait a minute. He owns the house. He bought it. Who am I to say, 'You may come in here now. I'm ready'?" Can you imagine selling your house, then living in it with all your stuff in one room after the new owner has moved in?

One thing is for sure: your thoughts will become more outward focused as you surrender ownership to the Father. There's not much to keep your eyes on when you own little.

One of the most important things we can do in life is find out what we were designed to be and do. But sometimes the answer escapes us because we may not be sure what the right question is. Author Henry Blackaby puts it like this: "'What is God's will for my life?' is not the best question to ask. I think the right question is simply, 'What is God's will?' Once I know God's will, then I can adjust my life to Him and His purposes."[3]

This adjusting of our lives has to do with the surrender of our wills to Jesus. It is total surrender. At key times when we experience that surrender—and I think it actually happens many times during our journey with Jesus—there is a complete shift from an inward focus to an outward one. Sometimes that shift is so subtle that it's nearly imperceptible, from "What do you want me to do?" to "I'm simply surrendered to your will, Jesus."

I remember prior to giving my life to Jesus, I would take walks at night around Cincinnati thinking about this. If it was really true what Christians were saying to me (and at that time they seemed to be popping up everywhere, like that Whack-a-Mole game in arcades—you get rid of one and another pops up), if it was really true that a personal God existed like they said, if it was really true that he sent his Son to die for me, then I had to respond in some way. I was so afraid of becoming weird, so afraid of becoming the stereotyped Christians I had created in my mind (although the stereotype was somewhat justified), that the idea of becoming like them was discombobulating. Yet at the same time, if it was true, there were grave consequences to my decision. I couldn't just ignore it. I was beginning to see that until I said yes to Jesus, every day I was saying no to God's design for my life. I had to adjust my life to him and his purposes.

Jesus called this "seeking first the kingdom of God and his righteousness" (see Matt. 6:33), and then he said everything else we need in life would be added to us. That's how outward he wants us to be.

There are some times (okay, a lot of times) when I've wrestled with the idea of finding God's will for my life. But lately I've tended to think it's less about finding and more about following. In other words, let's start with what we know generally, and we'll get to the specifics.

Sometimes we mistake God's plan for our lives for cracking a program code. Once we hack it, we download the program and simply use it. I've known people who have been trying to crack God's program for their lives for years. But doesn't the Bible say to seek? Yes, except the object of our search is Jesus and the kingdom, not some programmed clarity regarding what's going to happen in our lives. Real life flows out of relationship, not information. Solomon advises, "Trust God from the bottom of your heart; don't try to figure out everything on your own. Listen for God's voice in everything you do, everywhere you go; he's the one who will keep you on track" (Prov. 3:5–6 Message).

In his book *Ruthless Trust*, author Brennan Manning writes:

> When the brilliant ethicist John Kavanaugh went to work for three months at "the house of the dying" in Calcutta, he was seeking a clear answer as to how best to spend the rest of his life. On the first morning there he met Mother Teresa. She asked, "And what can I do for you?" Kavanaugh asked her to pray for him.
> "What do you want me to pray for?" she asked. . . .
> "Pray that I have clarity."
> She said firmly, "No, I will not do that." When he asked her why, she said, "Clarity is the last thing you are clinging to and must let go of." When Kavanaugh commented that she always seemed to have the clarity he longed for, she laughed and said, "I have never had clarity; what I have always had is trust. So I will pray that you trust God."[4]

God seems to give us just enough. One day at a time, not the whole plan. Just enough light for the next step. Jesus said, "This, then, is how you should pray: . . . 'Give us today our daily bread'" (Matt. 6:9, 11). Twelve-steppers have it right: one day at a time.

All we have to do is serve God and others. That's all I need to know today.

Clarity is not all it's cracked up to be.

Try something simple today.

Get a piece of paper out and cut it down to about the size of a business card. Write the following on one side of it: "This is just a simple way to say God loves you." On the other side, write the name of your church with the street address, the phone number, and the times of your services. Then, the next time you drive through a fast-food place, pay for the meal of the people in the car behind you and ask the cashier to give them your note. The cashier will smile. As you drive away, say a short prayer for the people behind you, such as, *Father, would you open up their hearts to receive all you have for them? Would you touch them through this with your love? And make them thirsty for the real food and the real drink, the ones that satisfy eternally.*

Just think if that happened all over your city today. Perhaps the climate would change.

Sometime back we got a letter that read, "Dear Vineyard, I just got back from McDonald's in Fairfield. It's Christmas Eve, and I literally counted change from couch cushions and my car to buy some lunch for my son. When I got to the window, the lady there told me that the man in front of me had paid for my food and had asked that she give me this card. It was a card from Vineyard. That man in front of me didn't know that I was a single mom, or that I'm not exactly the best, most sin-free person in the world." (I thought, *Gee, welcome to the church.*) "He just wanted me to know that God loved me. I needed this more than he could have possibly known. Regardless of what I get for Christmas this year, I will consider that reminder the best gift of all."

Isn't it amazing when the best gift of the year is nothing more than a Happy Meal?

You should write the name of your church on the paper not because of some marketing scheme for your church, but to give someone a chance to meet the beautiful body of Christ, that powerhouse community of wounded healers through whom God chooses to fulfill his plan.

Often we talk about surrendering our lives to Jesus Christ. But it strikes me that surrender is more of a process in three stages. The first stage is a surrender to survive. Jesus said, "Come to me, all you who are weary and burdened, and I will give you rest" (Matt. 11:28). In this surrender, we want help. We're beaten down. We're tired. Nothing else has worked. We want someone to save us. It's all about us at this stage—and appropriately so.

The next stage is a surrender to serve. It's here that we let God know we want to work for him, to serve his purposes. We want to express our gratitude in some way, to respond to the grace he's given us. It's not to earn anything from God; it's a gracious response to the gift of life from him.

After the 9/11 attack in New York, I read a news story about a woman on the fiftieth floor who somehow survived the towers' collapse. Although some people suffer from survivor guilt, this woman became totally filled with gratitude and purpose. She said, "I was spared for a reason. I want to serve God with all that is in me. I want to make a difference."

The last stage is a surrender to die. Jesus said, "Take up [your] cross and follow me" (Matt. 16:24). In other words, "Choose your form of execution and model your life after mine." That's not always being martyred for Jesus but rather dying daily—a death to self-will, to self-ambition, to recognition, to preference, to natural gifting, to everything in me that says there is a part of me that has to be protected. This is really radical. It's the part that other people won't understand . . . and the part we can't really talk about. It is humility on steroids. When a person is being crucified, they don't have any further plans. They aren't going anywhere anytime soon.

Out of these three levels of surrender comes a remarkable fruit, the one we're all looking for—the transformed life. And did you notice that life progressively moved from an inward focus to a totally outward one?

On a regular basis I get these questions: "Dave, when are we going to get the deep teaching? When am I going to get some meat here?" One night I snapped and came unglued on some poor guy who asked me that.

I asked, "Tell me who you think was the deepest teacher who ever existed. If anyone throughout history was going to do a Bible study, who would be the best teacher? Who would really know how to do it? Who knows exactly what human beings need to grow spiritually and can give them the best Grade A meat on the planet? Who would it be?"

These were rhetorical questions.

"I guess it would be Jesus," he replied.

"What is the largest collected sermon we have by Jesus? The Sermon on the Mount, Matthew 5–7. You read that and tell me what's deep there. This is Jesus's chance! If he's going to give us anything deep, here it is; let it rip!

"Read the Sermon on the Mount and tell me what's in it. Jesus is not doing some exegetical teaching of the tabernacles or the mandated feasts that all the male Jews had to attend. What did he talk about? 'Here's how you love each other; here's how you love God. Don't do this with God. Don't do this with each other; do that instead. Learn to forgive; learn to walk humbly; serve each other. Treat other people the way you want to be treated. Don't try to be a big shot in front of God; he sees it all. Do your prayers in secret.' And on and on.

"Tell me what's deep in that, please, and I'll do it. Every week."

We can't get around this love thing and we can't get around relationships, because what else are we going to love? It just doesn't get any deeper than us doing the things Jesus asked us to do. Remember? "You are my friends if you do what I command" (John 15:14). What is Jesus commanding? "Love each other as I have loved you" (v. 12). *Come on, there's got to be something more to it than that*, we may think. *Give me the meat, Jesus.*

The Bible says in John 4 that the disciples all went to get food, and when they came back they wondered if Jesus had already gotten a corned beef sandwich somewhere. Jesus said to them, "My food [meat] . . . is to do the will of him who sent me" (John 4:34). He had just spent time talking with a woman who had been married five times, was currently shacking up with a guy, and, what's more, was a Samaritan woman—the spiritual and racial untouchables in the Jews' eyes. He took the time and explained to her why her life was spiraling out of control, and that God, his Father, was looking for her and longing for her to draw near to him in real worship.

Funny thing: oftentimes I discover that when people are asking the "meat" question, they have never really involved themselves in evangelism—in touching the lives of the seekers and the clueless— which is the primary work of the church on earth to reveal the love of God. My life doesn't get any deeper than that.

I love studying and teaching about the prophetic feasts of Israel or the acrostic poetry of the Psalms or the meaning of the scarlet beast—my dream as a Christian introvert. But if they don't inspire compassion for others or a broken heart for the lost, I'm just on a theological head trip. As I understand it, when Jesus returns, he's not going to ask me if I taught on the premillenial significance of the Jubilee; rather, he's going to ask if I fed the hungry, invited strangers in, clothed the poor, laid hands on the sick, and visited those in prison. Call me crazy, but I think that's the meat God is looking for. And I have a hard enough time simply doing those things.

I know this is a simplistic approach. But sometimes simple is good. See if that doesn't fill you up.

Take this idea even further: if we were in God's perfect will, what would that look like? How would we know we were in his will? Do we have an assumed picture of what God's plan for us would look like? Does it mean that life's circumstances would all be favorable? Some single people might say they'd be married; some married people might say they'd be single! Would we have more money? Would we have different jobs? Would we be happier? Would we *feel* differently? I'm not trivializing; these are heartfelt, soul-searching questions. But when we start thinking about God's plan for our lives, we can have a lot of assumptions.

The story of Joseph is about a man who had all of his assumptions shattered. He was the favorite son growing up but was hated by his brothers. He was sold into slavery by them, was jailed on a trumped-up assault charge, and spent years in prison, but eventually he became the political savior of Egypt, developing a hugely successful welfare system during a national famine. Later Joseph said these words to his estranged brothers, the very ones who had sold him into slavery: "You intended to harm me, but God intended it for good to accomplish what is now being done, the saving of many lives" (Gen. 50:20).

David prayed, "I know, my God, that you test the heart" (1 Chron. 29:17). Jesus told his disciples that if they couldn't be trusted with the stuff of this earth, how would they handle the real treasures of the next world? We're all tested constantly. An average human being gets about 675,000 hours of pre-heaven testing.

God's will is pretty clear: he wants everyone to come to know him and to be changed into the likeness of his Son. As that happens, we'll see the world as Jesus saw it. His purpose will be our purpose. We'll love and serve the way Jesus loved and served.

The definition of a disciple is simple: a surrendered and transformed person who loves God and others. If God's will is transformed people who love God and others, our part is the surrender—he'll do the transformation.

I f you could use only five or six words, how would you describe yourself? You might say you're a student or the parent of two kids or a plumber or a spouse or whatever. Some of us may describe ourselves by what we do—an executive at Proctor & Gamble or a store manager at Taco Bell. At the beginning of the apostle Paul's most joyous letter, Philippians—which was written from prison—he begins with "Paul and Timothy, servants of Christ Jesus."

That word *servant* is derived from a Greek word that means "to bind," or someone bound to another person—a slave. The Greeks had two words for *slave*: someone who was captured in battle, or a person born into slavery. The latter is the word Paul uses here. He understood that prior to his conversion, he was a slave to himself, to the self-centered life. He was a servant to his own inward focus, or, in his own words, "a slave to sin" (Rom. 7:14). The New Testament states that we are all born into that slavery. We are not born virtuous—we are selfish, offensive people. That is our natural propensity.

If we're honest, we would all admit that sin is a hard taskmaster. I'm talking not about immoral behaviors but about a life that is lived independently of God's desires and the relationship he longs to have with us.

When Paul wrote that he was a servant or a slave to Jesus, he understood that by his new birth he was being bound to Jesus—and oddly enough, being a servant to this master was liberating.

What if we began to describe ourselves as servants—slaves—of Jesus Christ? How would that affect how we relate to others, especially those who don't yet know Jesus? It might make us completely free to serve them—those whom Christ has served by giving his life as a ransom. If he can do that, I'm sure I can serve those people.

Sometimes people will ask us how to get started doing these little acts of kindness in the name of Jesus. The beauty is that it doesn't take any training. Zero. Zilch. Nada. How skilled do you have to be to clean the toilet for free at a local business? As my friend Steve Sjogren once said, the most complicated maneuver is whether to swish clockwise or counterclockwise. And for some urban-myth reason, I tend to think that has something to do with which side of the equator you live on.

A few years ago I got the following email from someone who at that time had just become a believer. I had never met him personally.

> Today was fun. It was a normal workday in most senses, but I decided to do things a little differently. It was time to start serving people in the name of the Lord. I went to several different accounts for work today. I looked around and was able to locate a soda machine at a few of them. I made sure that no one was around, and I began purchasing some cans of pop. I rubber-banded a connect card from our church to each soda and placed them back into the dispenser slot. I noticed that pretty much every pop machine will allow three cans of soda to sit in the dispenser. $1.50 can show three people that God loves them! After I secretly placed the cans in the dispenser, I went on to my daily routines. I couldn't help but spy a little bit and check back to see if anyone had taken a soda. To my surprise, the sodas were gone almost immediately!
>
> As I was walking by, I saw a woman who looked like she was having a bad day. She grabbed one of the "free" sodas from the machine and began reading the connect card. She looked as if she had just been thrown a life preserver. I felt a lump in my throat immediately, and I had to turn away.
>
> I noticed today that this thing is more addictive than crack cocaine. I couldn't wait to do more and more of it. I ran up to the grocery store, and while walking by the quarter gumball machines, I had an idea. I set a connect card on the top of each machine and placed a quarter on every one of them. By the time I was leaving the grocery store, there was only one card left. I feel like I'm on

fire! I already invited a group to do the outreach on Saturday morning. This is the life Jesus promises!

Sincerely, Ryan

How simple is that? And that's not a bad addiction. But there's more to the story.

A few weeks ago I was on an outreach, heading to a Section 8 housing complex to hand out little boxes of Tide detergent. A youth group from another church in town had joined us. I didn't know their tattooed and pierced youth pastor, who teamed up with me. As we drove to the place, he told me that when he was younger, he was deep into partying, using drugs, living with his girlfriend, and being your basic hell-raiser.

But four different times he was approached by people who offered him a free bottle of water, washed his car, gave him a free Coke, etc. Four times. For months he hung on to the little card that was given to him, and finally he decided to check out the church.

It was there that he met Jesus after going through our Alpha program. And now he's serving in ministry as a youth pastor in another church, teaching students how to give their lives away in servanthood.

So as we were driving to the outreach he said to me, "I sent you an email years ago . . . about attaching cards to pop cans where I worked. My name is Ryan."

I love this stuff.

On September 30, 1938, the prime minister of England, Neville Chamberlain, announced to the British people that peace had been secured in Europe. He had met with Hitler and signed a peace agreement. It was a disastrous deal that carved up Czechoslovakia and gave part of it to Germany. And the chancellor of Czechoslovakia wasn't even part of the agreement! Within a few months, Hitler took the rest of Czechoslovakia, marched through Poland, and began bombing London.

When I got out of high school, I made minimum wage working in the shipping department of an upscale, overpriced furniture store. One day just before I quit working there, I wrapped a very expensive lamp in newspaper and conveniently left it outside on the dock near a pile of garbage, then I came back that night after everything was closed and stole it. I knew doing that was wrong but justified it with my conscience a dozen different ways. We can do that with pencils and paper clips from work. A few years later, something terrible happened: I became a Christian. After a while, that lamp began to bother me. So I did what any Christian would do—I put it in the closet.

Have you ever read the Edgar Allen Poe story "The Tell-Tale Heart," of the man who killed someone and buried him beneath the floor of his house? When the police came and talked to him, all he could hear in his mind was the heartbeat of the man he had murdered, until finally he confessed. Similarly, this lamp began to talk to me from the closet. And it said things like, "Put me back. I am not your lamp. What would Jesus do?" *Uh, in the first place, Jesus wouldn't have taken the lamp; he could have made one out of a fish or something.* But the lamp kept talking to me. Eventually I had to return it to the place I had taken it from, explaining that I had stolen it but had now become a Christian.

Chamberlain made a deal with the devil. When I stole that lamp, I made a deal with my devilish nature and justified it to myself. But there was no real peace in it. Have you ever tried to make a deal with your conscience?

Why should I forgive that person? They don't even want my forgiveness!

It doesn't matter if I fudge a little bit with my expense account— everyone does.

But I'm really lonely. What can it hurt if I cross some sexual boundary? Everyone expects that and does it.

I have a right to be angry. I have a right to self-pity. I have a right to get even. I have a right to be right!

Every day we make little deals. Inwardness can mean wanting comfort at any cost. Even the cost of our souls.

T rue Christianity is dynamic, not static.

In many ways, I think the church missed that truth. It remained static when the world shifted. The language changed, the music changed, and the media changed, and the church went into defense mode instead of missionary mode. Missionaries have outposts, not fortresses. Missionaries mix with the culture, not run from it. Missionaries love the people who are different from them, not hate them and call them names. Missionaries see their mission to heal, not defend. The reason we have cupholders in our chairs at the Vineyard is not for Christians to feel comfortable but for pre-Christians to feel relaxed in a family room, where they can see how a big, dysfunctional family is undergoing therapy with Jesus via the Holy Spirit. We can bring our coffee and come into the family room.

Jesus has a way of saying things that move us out of our comfort zones, out of the recliner with the built-in remote: "Here's another old saying that deserves a second look: 'Eye for eye, tooth for tooth.' Is that going to get us anywhere? Here's what I propose: 'Don't hit back at all.' If someone strikes you, stand there and take it. If someone drags you into court and sues for the shirt off your back, giftwrap your best coat and make a present of it. And if someone takes unfair advantage of you, use the occasion to practice the servant life. . . . Live generously" (Matt. 5:38–42 Message).

I can think of a dozen defensive statements for not living like that, things to do with justice, or fairness, or pain, or whatever. If you have abuse in your background, tread carefully here and listen to the whole message of Jesus. But in general, when you read that passage, do you think of other people who need to hear it? If so, look out. That's how you can tell if Jesus is about to throw out your recliner.

Jesus is all about comforting us, but that's different from making us comfortable. Serving others is not always comfortable, but who knows? Maybe we're bringing comfort to someone else.

Have you ever gone through times when God seems hidden? Usually it's at the worst of times. God just seems . . . not there. I believe there is a purpose for that. For the sake of growing and developing us, there are times when God seems simply to hide. The prophet Isaiah once wrote, "Truly you are a God who hides himself" (Isa. 45:15).

Christian philosopher and former atheist C. S. Lewis agonized over the death of his wife and kept a journal of his grief. This great defender of the Christian faith—the one who debated atheists and always seemed to have the answer for everything—had to suddenly wrestle with his own doubts. Shortly after his wife died of cancer he wrote, "Where is God? This is one of the most disquieting symptoms. . . . Go to Him when your need is desperate, when all other help is vain, and what do you find? A door slammed in your face, and a sound of bolting and double bolting on the inside. After that, silence. You may as well turn away. The longer you wait, the more emphatic the silence will become. There are no lights in the windows."[5]

It's nothing new. Thousands of years ago David wrote, "O LORD, why do you stand so far away? Why do you hide when I need you the most?" (Ps. 10:1).

It may be in the hiding that God forces us to change, to not look for him in well-worn ruts and paths, to admit our longing for him. He wants to be sought after, chosen. Could it be that like a lover's game of hard-to-get, God is creating in us a new desire for him? When the nation of Judah was stuck in captivity to the Babylonians, when circumstances were terrible, and when year after year passed, it was then that God spoke through Jeremiah to say, "'You will seek me and find me when you seek me with all your heart. I will be found by you,' declares the LORD" (Jer. 29:13–14).

God is there. Perhaps he's forcing our inwardness out. Perhaps he's getting us to look beyond ourselves, beyond our pain, to something outside: him.

We often talk about the sacrifice of Jesus. I believe he simply loved his Father more than he loved his own life. Loving God will cost you something. Love is never cheap, whether it's love for God, love for people, or even love of an ideal.

In the 1950s, Rosa was in love with the simple idea that everyone was born equal. In December 1955 in Montgomery, Alabama, after working a full day as a seamstress, Rosa was sitting on the bus in what was then called the colored section. A white man got on, but all the white seats were taken, so an entire row of African American riders were told to move for this one man. No one moved, including Rosa, until they heard these chilling words from the bus driver: "You all make it light on yourselves and let me have those seats." The passengers all moved except Rosa. She was arrested, fingerprinted, and thrown in jail. After she was released, she promptly went to work passing out leaflets to boycott riding the buses. A single day of protest turned into 381 days. Rosa received one death threat after another. She lost her job at the department store and had to move to Detroit to find work.

In 1963 she was one of thousands in Washington DC who heard her old friend Martin Luther King Jr. say, "I have a dream that one day on the red hills of Georgia the sons of former slaves and the sons of former slave owners will be able to sit down together at a table of brotherhood."

Rosa Parks was a follower of Jesus. Her favorite book was the Bible, and she stood many a time on her favorite passage: "The Lord is the strength of my life; of whom shall I be afraid?" (Ps. 27:1 NKJV). In an interview years later she was asked if she was afraid when she took a stand on the bus. She said, "I have learned over the years that when one's mind is made up, this diminishes fear."[6]

What if we expressed our love for God like that? What sacrifices would we make? What sacrifices have we made lately in expressing our love for God? Perhaps it's an emotional one—the need to be right in some argument. Perhaps it's a financial issue. If we've not found something to sacrifice for, we've not found anything to love.

Over the years I've heard numbers of people say, "When I get to heaven, I'm going to have a lot of questions for God!" I'm not so sure we're going to feel like that when we get there.

As I read about the life of Jesus, I discover that he asked a lot of questions. He even had that annoying habit of answering a question with a question. But here's the difference—we ask questions to get answers, but God asks questions to lead us toward self-discovery. Remember, he already knows all the answers.

Here's my observation: the things I discover in my heart force me to own up to them and do something about them. For instance, someone may tell me that I'm a jerk, but that really won't mean as much as if one day I realize, "Hey, I'm a jerk!" With self-awareness come ownership and the opportunity for me to really change.

God asks questions to help us grow in our sense of self-discovery and therefore grow toward him as well. The questions God asks are deeply personal and probe two primary areas: my motivations (why do I do the things I do?) and my values (what do I really think is important?). If we read the Bible closely, we'll see that God was always asking questions that delved into those two points. And he does that to you and me on a daily basis.

Here's the big picture: God's overall purpose is that he wants to draw us to himself. It's in him that we find our life, our wholeness. Now here's the problem: we have to choose. While love is the only vehicle to true intimacy, God cannot force us to love him. So he gives us continual choices to help us uncover what our real motivations are and what we really value in life.

Today we can choose to be either rebels or servants of God. I think ultimately those are our only two options. We had best choose wisely—and start practicing.

Years ago we took our kids to a community pool that had a high diving board. I'm not much of a swimmer; if there was an Olympic trial for dog-paddling, I could be a contender. But one time I told my wife, Anita, that I was going to do the high board. I remember climbing up the ladder and thinking, *This can't be that bad.*

But after walking out on the diving board, I realized, *Whoa. What was I thinking?* The pool looked like a postage stamp. What's worse, I couldn't just jump in; I had to dive to look good. I was contemplating all this—scared to death because I don't like heights—and wondering how long people would laugh if I crawled back across the board and climbed down, when suddenly some ten-year-old kid standing at the top step of the ladder behind me said, "Are you going to go or not?"

You know how you jump on the board to get a good bounce? Well, that didn't happen. I just kind of walked off. But it was a perfect swan dive—that is, if someone had shot the swan first. There's nothing like a good belly flop from a high board. When I got out of the water, it looked like I had a serious sunburn.

It took me a good while to go back up on the high board. But eventually I did—and it was the beginning of a great summer of bad diving. But fun.

Most of us have belly flopped in life. We took a risk on the high board—in a relationship, a career change, a new location, or what we thought was a chance on God—and then something didn't work out. It's hard to get back up on the high board.

But you have to. You weren't made for one dive. What if, when you were learning how to walk, you had given up the first time you fell down? Don't let your life be determined by your last failure. Don't let anyone else write the last page of your book. That's God's business—and yours to discover.

Get back on the diving board. Serve God, serve others.

At one time I had my Christian life neatly prioritized: first, God; second, family; third, work. And then I prioritized those categories into subcategories. For instance, under "family" would be wife, then kids, then bloodline family, extended family, some relatives in Kentucky, Lucy the family dog, some of the other relatives in Kentucky, my wife's Uncle Frank in northern Ohio, and so on.

The problem is that all the categories are interrelated. It's God in my family, God in my work, God in serving God. By loving my family, I worship God and honor him. I work in order to give to others and think of that as giving to God himself. We pigeonhole and categorize; God integrates and makes whole. We see either/or; God sees both/and. Jesus blurs the line between what we might call the sacred and the secular.

In a fascinating parable about the separation of the sheep from the goats (Matt. 25:31–46), the astonishing thing is that the sheep are genuinely surprised that they really did anything directly to Jesus. He helps them understand that when they did anything for the least, they were doing that to God. They were people who went to their graves never knowing they had ministered to Jesus, perhaps never knowing how he was a part of everything, in both the exhilarating times and the mundane routine.

It may very well be that God is more interested in the routine of our lives than the big spiritual explosions that occur from time to time. It's like when we suddenly realize, *Oh, so when I love my wife, it's an act of love toward God? I get it.* It's in the routine, not the big heroic moments, that our true character is exposed. That would be like me, a horrible volleyball player, one day having a good game and then foolishly saying, "Now you're seeing the real Dave Workman."

Focusing on living for God enables you to stop defining your life by your activities. So the next time you're at a party and someone asks, "What do you do for a living?" you can say, "I love God." That'll liven up the party.

C an you imagine a marriage that is conflict free? That's ridiculous. Conflict doesn't invalidate a relationship; it only expands our commitment to love. It expands our dependence on Jesus. It cuts to the core of who we are—how are we becoming Christlike in that relationship? It's only in relationships that we have the opportunity to find out what Jesus would do.

When the New Testament talks about the church, it always has an eschatological view—that is, there is a future purpose for the church. Because of that, we see our current needs and differences in a different light. If I thought that all justice was going to be derived through the current courts and legal systems in the United States, I'd be one depressed dude.

You can sense Paul's frustration when he finds out that folks in the Corinthian church were taking each other to court over arguments. He writes, "If any of you has a dispute with another, dare he take it before the ungodly for judgment instead of before the saints? Do you not know that the saints will judge the world? And if you are to judge the world, are you not competent to judge trivial cases? Do you not know that we will judge angels? How much more the things of this life!" (1 Cor. 6:1–3).

In other words, if we can't figure out how to settle issues between ourselves here, how in the world will we be able to rule and reign with Jesus Christ? When Paul starts using pie-in-the-sky language, it's because he knows we have to learn how to bake the pie here first. Do we think that when we die and walk into the light of immortality, we are suddenly going to be conflict-free, nice people? I believe that when the Scripture says we shall be changed (1 Cor. 15:51), it's referring to our bodies, not our psychological makeup.

Let's get real: who wants to end up as a servant? There is a certain amount of fleshly enjoyment in rolling around in our self-centeredness. But there is nothing of that in heaven. This is not the rehearsal. This is where our Christlikeness is formed. This time on earth is where our character—who we are—is built.

Sometimes people ask me how to find time to do outward-focused activities. They say, "Yeah, I'd like to wash cars for free, or visit a nursing home, or pass out free bottles of water . . . but I work fifty hours a week, and I have kids with school functions and sports, and I go to church and even have a small group, not to mention trying to fit in some quiet time and Bible reading. I just can't add another thing to my list!"

I can agree with that. Sometimes there are seasons for certain things. And I'm assuming that all of us are attempting to prioritize our activities based on our values and maximize our time. But maybe we compartmentalize a bit too much.

I was reading a local Cincinnati magazine the other day when I came across a picture of a family from our church—Tres and Paula Kutcher and their three kids. Paula said that taking part in practical outreaches is a lifestyle for their family. She said, "It's enjoyable to be stepping outside the box of ourselves and doing for others. It's good for the children to see that, and they enjoy it, too." The whole family wraps gifts for free with the Vineyard at the local mall. Their oldest son loves to help his dad shovel snow from other people's driveways. It seems the Kutchers don't see having an outward focus as one more thing to squeeze in; they simply incorporate it as part of their regular family time. And what an amazing way to show kids that life is not all about them, especially during the Christmas season.

The article said that daughter Hannah loves to give away hot chocolate for free to shoppers during the holidays. She said, "I like that we get to taste the hot chocolate. It's fun to be with my friends and family doing this. And it's funner to be giving the hot chocolate away than to be getting it."

Didn't Jesus say something like that once? That it's "funner" to give than to receive? What a great, real-life way to show your kids one of the greatest secrets of the kingdom of God.

And it's funner.

Availability

Awhile back we had a youth group from Michigan visiting and going on outreaches with us. They were sent to a nursing home to just spend some time talking with senior citizens. A student named Tim, soon to be a ninth grader, overheard someone in a nearby room say, "There isn't much time." He looked into the room and saw an entire family gathered around someone in the bed. Tim called his youth leader to come over and said, "We need to pray for these people!" She encouraged him to lead the way.

Tim went into the room, introduced himself to the family, and asked if it would be okay if he prayed for the man and for them. He explained that the group was not even from Cincinnati, but he believed that God sent them to be there for that family at that particular moment, because that's how much God cared for them. They were all stunned, and one person said, "I think Dad would really like it if we prayed." So fresh-out-of-eighth-grade Tim led the group in prayer . . . and there wasn't a dry eye in the room.

But here's the best part. Two days later Tim happened to be at another outreach on the other side of town, passing out water bottles. A car stopped, the window rolled down, and some guy took the water—and then he yelled, "Oh my God! You're the kid who prayed for my father a couple of days ago. Thanks so much!" While he was waiting at the light, he told Tim that his father passed away, but it meant so much to get this water today from Tim, of all people.

Here's the deal: God is looking for available people. Not super skilled. Not super clever. Not even with a super-huge life experience. You don't have to have the high-powered testimony of "I was on crack for twenty years and now I'm screwed up on Jesus." You only have to be available.

And he'll take a thirteen-year-old.

When you think about it, the invasion of this planet by God himself in the form of a tiny baby born on the other side of the tracks is remarkably subtle. But it wasn't so subtle for a young Jewish girl named Mary. After she got over an angel named Gabriel scaring the daylights out of her—and by the way, have you ever noticed that angels always start off with "Don't panic"?—she responded with an open heart: "I am the Lord's servant, and I am willing to accept whatever he wants" (Luke 1:38 NLT). Mary was an ordinary person distinguished by her availability.

God is not looking for skilled people. He's not looking for the highest IQs. He's not looking for superstars. I find it interesting when people say, "Wouldn't it be great if so-and-so became a Christian—they are so talented." God doesn't need talent. He doesn't need slick salesmen. He just needs people who say, "I am willing." He's looking for availability. He's looking for a room in our hearts in which to be born. That's all. He'll take a stable. And honestly, that's what most of us are. We think we're the Hilton, but we're all just a Motel 6.

Martin Luther King Jr. once wrote, "Everybody can be great because anybody can serve. You don't have to have a college degree to serve. You don't have to make your subject and verb agree to serve. . . . You only need a heart full of grace; a soul generated by love."[1]

How available are you? It's amazing how many times in the Bible we read this simple responsive prayer: "Here I am."

When God called to Abraham to test him, Abraham responded with, "Here I am."

When the angel of God spoke to Jacob in a dream, Jacob said, "Here I am."

When Moses was stunned by the sight of an unconsumed burning bush, he said, "Here I am."

When Isaiah was overwhelmed by the wonder of God, he said, "Here I am. . . . Send me."

In a prophetic passage regarding the Messiah who was to come, God spoke to Isaiah, saying, "My people shall know My name; therefore in that day I am the one who is speaking, 'Here I am'" (Isa. 52:6 NASB).

The wonder of the incarnation is that God made himself available to us. Can we have any other response than to give our own availability?

Recently we were on an outreach in a neighborhood of Cincinnati that's been depressed economically for a number of years. We visit there on a regular basis doing different small things. On this Saturday morning, with a pickup truck full of groceries from Costco, we walked around and knocked on doors, asking whoever answered if they knew anyone who could use some free groceries. Almost everyone gratefully received the groceries themselves. It was a simple little touch, that's all. But the best thing was what followed: we always asked if there was anything we could pray for with them. The kingdom comes with the practical and the power.

We knocked on the first door of a rundown, rickety building of peeled paint, torn screens blowing in the wind, plastic-wrapped windows, and warped wood. A young pregnant woman answered. We introduced ourselves, and she said her name was Sherrie. She gladly took the groceries. When we asked if we could pray for her, she said, "I'm due in nineteen days. I just want everything to go okay. I'm really nervous." I asked if this was her first baby and she said yes. So there we all stood in the doorway on a cold January morning and prayed for her delivery, her doctors, her nurses, her baby, and, of course, her nerves. When we finished and started to leave, Sherrie suddenly said, "Would you rub your hand on my stomach?" Maybe she thought there was something magical about this gray-haired guy who had just prayed.

In all my years of attempting to learn the art of serving, I think that was a first for me: being asked by a perfect stranger—from a different socioeconomic demographic, who was a different race and a different gender—to rub my hand on her stomach.

But of course I did. And prayed for a little unborn child about to come into a world of immense challenges. *God, bring your kingdom . . . and everything will be alright.*

Sherrie smiled and thanked us and closed the door. And for a brief moment, all the walls came down and all was calm in this part of the universe . . . as it is in heaven.

Have you ever had any missed opportunities in your life? At one point some folks I know were invited to invest a little bit of money in a new hamburger franchise starting in Columbus. They turned it down. They probably figured, *Do we need another McDonald's chain?* Now Wendy's International owns nearly ten thousand restaurants worldwide.

In the early 1600s, the Dutch government bought Manhattan from a native tribe for about twenty-four dollars. P. Diddy once sold his Park Avenue townhouse for seventeen million dollars. But that's nothing: an apartment at One Central Park sold for forty-two million dollars.

In the 1960s, every major record label in England turned down a little band in Liverpool called the Beatles. One of the largest record company executives told the Beatles' manager that "music groups with guitars are over."

Sometimes I think about the amazing story of the separation of the sheep from the goats that Jesus told in Matthew's Gospel. The righteous "sheep" asked, "Lord, when did we see you hungry and feed you, or thirsty and give you something to drink? When did we see you a stranger and invite you in, or needing clothes and clothe you? When did we see you sick or in prison and go to visit you?" (Matt. 25:37–39). Jesus responded, "I tell you the truth, whatever you did for one of the least of these brothers of mine, you did for me" (v. 40). Did you get that? They never knew they were doing ministry to Jesus, that they were actually serving him, loving him.

I have a feeling that every day there are little opportunities I miss that are big invitations to serve the King of Kings, that the Creator of the universe was hidden behind the smallest act of love I could have expressed to someone. One act of servanthood—no matter if it's as small as a cup of water offered . . . or a water bottle . . . or possibly even a Diet Coke on a street corner—has a spiritual impact that is greater than we could possibly imagine.

Just being a servant means something special to God.

For what it's worth, I'm a serious introvert. And not just an introvert but extremely capable of being a wickedly self-centered introvert. That's why developing some outward-focused habits and regularly asking Jesus to remind me that my new heart beats with his mercy are important to put in my schedule. I forget easily.

But from time to time I remember that a key to this kingdom life is just being open and available, not necessarily gifted or clever. Recently I was at Taco Bell, and as I was leaving, out of the blue I thought I heard God say to me, *Tell the man sitting at that table that I said he's a good father.* I looked back and saw a young guy with some piercings and tattoos sitting at a table with a little three- or four-year-old girl and a baby in a stroller.

I swallowed hard, walked over, and said, "Wow, you've got some beautiful kids." He didn't even look up but just mumbled, "Thanks." I said, "You know, I'm not really a crazy person, but I was just getting ready to leave here and felt like God said to tell you you're a good father."

There was a pause, then he looked up at me, his eyes teared up, he smiled, and he said, "I'm trying really hard."

I said, "Well, I think God thinks you're doing a good job."

Wouldn't it be amazing if we could actually see people the way God sees them? I think somehow we've gotten the idea that the only emotions God feels are either some sappy sentimentalism or perpetual crankiness about us messing up his world and rearranging the furniture. I think he's thrilled with any small steps anyone takes toward wanting to do the right thing. It's not a salvation by works, but maybe it reveals a heart that at its core is seeking God—and doesn't even know it yet.

If you're moving toward developing an outward-focused lifestyle, try this: buy a venti mochaccino and just walk around a shopping mall. Then ask God to give you his heart for his lost children.

And be prepared.

When we talk about serving people who don't yet know Jesus, let's make sure we don't miss the supernatural aspect of what is happening: God is already drawing and wooing and convicting and working in the lives of people every day, people who cross our paths. We probably have too small a view of the kingdom of God and can't see that he is ahead of all of us, moving in the lives of people day in and day out. And all he wants to do is use us in his supernatural movement in others' lives. He wants to write some divine appointments into our PDAs and Outlook calendars.

I went to a shopping plaza with some out-of-town high school students to give away bags of candy to employees of small businesses. We had split up into several teams, and as I was walking with my group, two of the kids came running out of a little gift shop, screaming, "Pastor Dave, Pastor Dave, this woman wants directions to your church . . . and we don't know where we are!" I walked into the shop and found the manager with moist eyes. She said to me, "God must really be after me." When she became a teenager, she left a cult in which she had grown up. Recently someone had given her a book about the end times, and she was reading it since business was slow. But she was getting totally freaked out and wondered—at that very moment—if God really loved her. Suddenly, in walked some high school students who gave her a bag of candy and said to her—and I'm not making this up—"We just want you to know that God loves you."

That's a divine appointment. That's the supernatural element of God using us when we decide to simply be available and connect with people by serving them in some simple way. Coincidence? Maybe, but as one person has said, a coincidence is when God does a miracle but chooses to remain anonymous. I've been walking with Jesus for over thirty years and have had a boatload of coincidences.

One more thing. Maybe I'm a little biased here, but it seems to me that I've had way more of those little supernatural coincidences when I'm serving lost people than any other time. Try checking out that stat for yourself.

Recently there was a psychic fair in our city's convention center. Psychics, mediums, alternative healers, and others set up booths to sell and promote their stuff and charge for their services. Sometimes in these types of situations, Christians protest with bullhorns, telling people they're going to hell. We agree that the Bible says mediums and divination are not kosher, but we took a different approach: we got a booth inside. Karin Maney and Kande Wilson, directors of prayer and evangelism respectively, joined forces and arranged to get a booth in the fair with a cool banner that said "Healing Prayer and Dream Interpretation."

I asked Karin, "I know we regularly pray for sick people, but do we know how to interpret dreams?"

Karin smiled and replied, "Uh, well, we're learning fast."

Why not? God has all power and knows what's coming up, so we'll just pray our usual prayer: "Oh God, oh God, oh God . . . help!"

But the funniest part was that our booth was free, which of course created problems with the other vendors who were charging for their services. (They're psychics—they should have seen that coming.) And to top it off, we gave away fortune cookies. No kidding. Of course, we had our own fortunes printed inside them. Some were simple Scriptures, quotes from books, or things such as, "If you don't know where you're going, any road will take you there." I thought it was funny to have fortune cookies at a psychic fair.

Some of our volunteer team members who worked the booth sent me emails afterward. One wrote about a man who came up to the booth and "asked for prayer for healing for his back. When we prayed, heat began to radiate all down his back. He said it was coming through the top of his head and through his back. He received total relief for his pain! . . . Shortly after that he brought back a couple more of his friends so we could pray for them."

My friend Ken Glassmeyer said, "It was like fishing with dynamite. Now I know how Simon Peter felt when Jesus told him to row out just a bit farther and lay down his nets! When can we do this again?"

The power of God showed up at that fair, and many experienced the kingdom of God for the first time. Remember, Jesus died for them. And lots of those attending the fair were what we call "God seekers."

They just don't know the God who is looking for them.

One of my favorite accounts in the Bible is the story of Gideon. Gideon is a guy I can relate to: he's scared and doubtful of seeing God move on his behalf, and he has a big, dysfunctional family. That's my kind of guy.

We meet Gideon when he's hiding out in a winepress while threshing his grain because he's afraid of the Midianites, who have invaded the Israelites' land. An angel shows up and says, "The Lord is with you, mighty warrior."

Gideon says, "Yeah, right. It looks to me like God abandoned us. Why isn't he sending us a deliverer like he did way back in Egypt?"

The angel responds, "He is. That's why I'm here. And you're the man . . . you big, bad soldier you." (See Judges 6.)

Gideon needed more persuasion. And he had a half-baked, scaredy-cat start with God's first assignment—tearing down the family idol. People who are called to do truly great things rarely think they can do truly great things.

In response to an article in the *London Times* called "What's Wrong with the World?" Catholic philosopher and author G. K. Chesterton wrote a letter to the editor that said simply, "Dear sirs, I am. Yours truly, G. K. Chesterton."

We're the problem . . . and the solution. God's answer to fix whatever is broken is always going to be a person—and almost always a person who doesn't think he or she can do it. Our friend Doug Roe moved to Dayton, Ohio, to plant a church. He was working in a grocery store to support himself while trying to get the church started, just scratching out a living. One day he was sweeping the floor when he overheard a woman telling someone that her car had broken down and she didn't have any money to fix it. Doug prayed quietly, *God, please help that woman. Send someone across her path who can help her.* He said he instantly heard the voice of the Holy Spirit say, *That's you, Doug. That's why I sent you to Dayton.*

Doug began doing free oil changes in his driveway, buying the oil himself. Even better, he didn't know anything about cars. Once he accidentally spilled a pan of used oil on the head of a person who was looking under his car.

I think that's why I like this servant stuff. You don't need to be brave. You don't need to be smart. You don't need to have it all together. You just need to have a desire to serve some lost soul with a little bit of love and a whole lot of grace, which God seems to supply in abundance.

How simple is that?

Often it seems a lot of evangelism training is focused on knowing all the answers to every possible question people might ask us. And sometimes we Christians think we actually have to have all the answers. But doesn't it drive you crazy when someone thinks they're always right and wants to make sure you know it? Even if by some miracle they were always right, if the messenger comes off as self-righteous, you never learn the lesson.

A simple "Gee, I don't know . . ." goes a long way toward building a relationship that hopefully will allow me to speak the grace and truth of Jesus into someone's heart. I love the Message paraphrase of Jeremiah 23:37: "Don't pretend that you know all the answers yourselves and talk like you know it all. I'm telling you: Quit the 'God told me this . . . God told me that . . .' kind of talk."

Even though Jesus seemed to know everything and could see into peoples' hearts, the Bible says he was meek and humble of heart. There are times when I'm meeting with someone that I'm mentally rehearsing what I'm going to say the entire time they're talking. I'm too busy waiting for my turn to talk.

I've been wondering lately how all my conversations would shift if I had no agenda other than being used by God in a servant manner to listen—a no-strings-attached approach. What a change that would make in my conversations!

The Bible has so many things to say about the way we relate to others and the way we share our love of Jesus. Proverbs 18:13 says, "Answering before listening is both stupid and rude" (Message). One of the simplest ways of serving someone outside the body of Christ is to listen to them rather than slam your view into them. Of course we need to be able to give a defense of our faith, but oftentimes I think we can come across more offensive than defensive.

Try a little servant listening; see what happens when you serve someone with your heart . . . and your ears.

L et me give you an outward-focused slant on prayer. In prayer, the depth of my submission is exposed. Christian philosopher C. S. Lewis wrote, "We must lay before Him what is in us, not what ought to be in us."[2] Prayer is the honest admission of what we are and what we don't want to do, and then relinquishing that to him. Prayer always probes the depth of our submission; it allows God to dip his bucket into the pool of our hearts and bring up things that are too deep for us to find, both good and bad.

The Bible records three fascinating prayers of Jesus within a twenty-four-hour period. At the Last Supper, Jesus took a cup of wine and gave thanks to God for the cup that represented the supreme act of sacrifice—his own innocent blood for those who would reject him. He was saying thanks for that sacrificial opportunity.

But within a matter of hours in the Garden of Gethsemane, Jesus prayed, "Father, if it is possible, may this cup be taken from me" (Matt. 26:39). What had been accepted with thanks just hours earlier was now received with such agony that Jesus sweat drops of blood. The prayer was answered with a no from his Father. There was only one course of action to take—to submit to the Father's will, not his own.

And then, after being beaten, whipped, spit upon, stripped, and nailed to a cross for six gut-wrenching hours, Jesus cried out, "My God, my God, why have you forsaken me?" (Matt. 27:46). At this point, Jesus is not hearing anything from the Father. There is no response to his cry.

Submission means that our personal agendas, our personal missions, and what we want out of life have to be under God's mission. The prefix *sub* means "under." Our desires, our mission, have to be under God's.

Sometimes prayer is communicating to God what we want, but then accepting what he wants. His will, not ours. In my case, God has a plan for Cincinnati, for his church, and for my life and how it intersects with what he's doing here.

That's an outward-focused prayer.

D avid once said, "I will not sacrifice to the Lord my God burnt offerings that cost me nothing" (2 Sam. 24:24). If we are to become servants and give expression to the life of Jesus in us, there will be a cost. But the return is always bigger than the investment.

One of my wife's friends sent us this story:

> The day before Thanksgiving I had to go to the store and pick up a few items. As I was leaving, I heard the Lord say, *Wait, Connie. I have someone I need you to bless today.*
>
> As I watched the lines, an older woman was placing her items on the counter. She looked like a great-grandmother. I saw six out-of-control children behind her. When her groceries were bagged, she swiped her card through the welfare machine. The card wouldn't go through, and the clerk called the manager. They all tried, but it was declined. The manager and clerk became very frustrated, and I overheard him say, "Now we have to put all these items back on the shelf."
>
> I approached the woman and said, "Today Jesus is paying for your groceries." She looked shocked and said, "Oh no, please."
>
> I said, "The Lord has given me instructions; he would like to bless you today."
>
> When I saw all the groceries, I feared I wouldn't have enough money. When all was done, the bill came to $77.82—exactly how much I had in my pocketbook . . . to the penny. I almost cried right then. I hugged her and heard one of the children say, "We're going to have Thanksgiving, huh, Granny?"
>
> I was really shaking by this time. As I drove out of the parking lot, I caught a glimpse of the woman holding her hands to the sky and giving thanks. What a great Thanksgiving I had this year!
>
> Love, Connie

Isn't it amazing, when our outward-focused antenna is up, how God can use us? And there is no better feeling in the world than to know that the God of the universe has just tapped on your shoulder for his purposes.

Regardless of the cost.

Besides our kids carrying our genes and being recipients of our love, which runs deeper than we would have ever guessed, they are also a discipleship gift to us. How many disciples do you have that live with you day in and day out for eighteen years?

I remember hearing Tony Campolo speak about the number one thing that parents in the United States want for their children: for them to be happy. There is something really sad about that, to just be happy. What about being self-sacrificial? What about being courageous despite pain? What about being responsible? What about being God lovers? What about just being loving in general?

Sometimes I read the words of Jesus and think, *No one teaches like that—and really means it or lives it.* The kingdom of God is so radically different that it's hard for us to put into practice even the simplest things. It's as if everything we've ever been taught is turned upside down.

For a couple of years I ran a two-minute radio spot called "An Outward-Focused Thought" on a local Christian radio station. I would end each spot with this: "Let's make a difference in someone's life today. . . . Let's go serve somebody." Later a listener emailed the station the following:

> I drive my ten-year-old son to school with arrival time between 8:00 and 8:15. I had heard several of Dave's spots and really liked them. Though it is typically a time that my son and I talk on the way to school, I have been turning on the radio to hear what Dave has to say, a daily pick-me-up. My son heard one, and now we are scheduling our leaving time so we can ensure that he gets to hear it. . . . When my kids get home from school, I have always asked them two questions from a talk I once heard. First, what was the best thing that happened to you? And second, what did you do to help someone today? Last week when I picked my son up from school, he jumped in the car and said, "Do you want to know how I served someone today?" I guess I will start asking that question instead.

It got me wondering how our kids would turn out if that was the daily question: how did you serve someone today?

Recently I was with a group doing an outreach down in the West End projects. We were offering some groceries to people and then asking if we could pray for them. I remember a few times when my wife and I were first married and scraping by on dimes, and someone offered us a gift certificate for somewhere; that meant so much to us. We wouldn't buy a carton of Cokes because that was a luxury, so a little gift really meant a lot. Same thing with this outreach—just a little bonus. But the real deal is inviting the Holy Spirit to come.

I was sitting in a dark apartment with an eighty-year-old woman named Shirley who just wanted to talk for a while. She had moved to Cincinnati over twenty years ago but didn't have any family left. Recently she had a cataract operation that went badly, and she lost the sight in her right eye. Now her other eye had a cataract, and Shirley said, "They aren't touching this one!"

She told us that a few years ago, while standing on the street corner, she was shot in the stomach—a stray bullet from a drive-by. I thought about my mom and what a traumatic experience that would be. Shirley said that God had been good to her and had kept her all these years. She said, "I've got angels in the bushes, honey."

I smiled and thought, *Whoa, Shirley. I haven't seen any bushes around here for blocks. It's all concrete!* We talked for a while longer and then prayed. Shirley hugged us all and thanked us for sitting with her.

As I got up to leave, Shirley focused her one half-good eye on me and said, "Honey, you're one of those angels." I thought about that on the car ride home. My friends who know me well know I'm no angel, and I'm sure deep down Shirley knows that too. But as the writer of Hebrews said, "Don't forget to show hospitality to strangers, for some who have done this have entertained angels without realizing it!" (Heb. 13:2 NLT).

I know I'm not an angel, but an eighty-year-old woman who can take a bullet . . . she might be.

My friend Don Eichorn told me a great story about Halloween. He used to love Halloween and would dress up like Frankenstein—with homemade six-foot-long shoes—and scare everyone who came to his house. His neighbors would all sit on their porches to watch the show.

And then Don became a Christian. After learning more about Halloween, he decided to have nothing to do with what he considered a "satanic" holiday. But recently he said, "I still believe that the enemy has special practices specific to that night, but I guess I've decided that I'm not willing to give him even one night without a fight."

In the last five years Don has been giving away the biggest and best candy bars in the neighborhood. On every candy bar he attaches a short message such as "God loves you!" He also sets up a movie screen in his driveway, where he shows Christian music videos and movies like *Finding Nemo*.

But a few years ago Don pushed the envelope. He gathered some friends and set up a "Prayer Table" on the sidewalk. He had index cards that guests could write their requests on, which he and his friends prayed for later, and he had six friends available to pray for people on the spot. They were shocked by the response: over fifty people filled out cards, and the group prayed with lots of people right on the street!

One twenty-year-old man said, "I don't even know what prayer is." They explained it to him and then prayed over him. It was probably the first time in his life he heard someone pray specifically for him, while several of his friends stood waiting close by.

Don said, "We had cards filled out that ranged from 'Make my brother not be so mean' to 'Please pray that I don't kill myself tonight.' We caught a glimpse of what God wants to do in our city—bring good news to the poor, set the captives free, restore sight to the blind."

Maybe that feels a little too risky for you. It's pretty radical. But you've got to love it when someone takes something dark and shines the Light on it.

Generosity

Have you ever played the lottery? The stats are pretty good that you can do just as well if you throw your money out the car window. Once someone asked me, "Dave, what do you believe about gambling?" I said, "Depends what you believe about tithing." Hey, I'm just trying to be an honest pastor.

A while back we challenged people in our church with the Outward-Focused Life Lottery. It was way cool! Everyone got a scratch-off lottery ticket, but instead of an amount of money on it that they won, there was an outreach they got to do, such as buy a neighbor a pizza. Or sponsor a free dog wash in their neighborhood. Or buy someone's movie tickets. Or the big one: fill up the gas tank of the person at the pump next to you. The lottery ticket also had some cards attached to it to explain to someone that this was just a simple way of saying that God knows them and loves them. A number of letters came in, like this one:

> Well, I don't know where to start. My fiancé and I are struggling. I mean really struggling to the point we are being evicted from our apartment. We have no money to pay our rent, and our van is an old clunker that my ex-husband sold us for $60. We still owe $30 on that. My fiancé's mom gave us $20 today to put in the gas tank so I can get to and from work a couple of days (I work in a nursing home). Well, anyway, I put the whole $20 in the tank, knowing we had no food at home. . . . Right now the gas is more important to us. So after we put the $20 in the gas tank we were broke again. Well, out of nowhere came a lady and said, "Ma'am, God loves you and wants you to have this to help with your gas," and she walked away. She also handed me a card with the church name on it. We were able to get some food because of that $20. I want to say thank you from the bottom of our hearts. . . . She came and went like an angel and found us at the BP gas station on Mitchell Ave. Thank you so much.
>
> Judy and Bill

How simple is that? And even though it's hard to find a theological basis for angels with reverse lottery tickets, you have to admit that's pretty cool.

One of the marks of the outward-focused life is simple generosity. Generosity is such a powerful virtue, so winsome, so easy for anyone to understand. I'm convinced that generosity is a spiritual force that affects people at a spiritual level, simply because it reflects the generous heart of the Father. Jesus constantly hammered his disciples on this: "Now that I've put you there on a hilltop, on a light stand—shine! Keep open house; be generous with your lives. By opening up to others, you'll prompt people to open up with God, this generous Father in heaven" (Matt. 5:16 Message).

I'm convinced this is the lost power of the church. In the second century there was a popular satirist named Lucian. He disliked all religions and called Christians "wretches." But one thing caught him off guard. Regarding Christianity, he wrote, "It is incredible to see the ardor with which the people of that religion help each other in their wants. They spare nothing. Their first legislator has put into their hearts that they are all brethren."[1] Just think of that: more than one hundred years after Jesus was crucified, there was historical evidence that the words of Jesus still rang true—"By this all men will know that you are my disciples, if you love one another" (John 13:35).

There is a power in generosity, a power to live above the scratching and clawing of this world. Generosity is the ultimate evidence of a person who is really free. It's both the fruit of a free person and the pathway to freedom itself. Although often attributed to Winston Churchill, it was Ronald Reagan who said, "We make a living by what we get; we make a life by what we give."[2]

Try something this week: With each decision you make, stop and ask this simple question: *Jesus, am I being generous or stingy?* And don't forget that we can be stingy with more than our money—we dole out our time, our abilities, our forgiveness, and our love.

In her book *The Overspent American*, Juliet Schor noted a recent study showing that each hour per week in front of the TV corresponds with an average consumption increase of over two hundred dollars a year. It's estimated that by the time an American reaches twenty years old, he or she will have seen one million commercial messages in print or on video. Teenagers are the fastest-growing consumer demographic, spending about 150 billion dollars yearly. It's the job of advertisers not just to inform you of what you need, but to create needs you didn't know you had. This is a culture that has produced the Abdomenizer, Chia Pets, the Clapper, and the Thighmaster.

At our house, we have the cheapest cable package offered: it's basically ABC, CBS, NBC, Fox, local cable access, and thirteen Home Shopping Network–type channels. Something is not right.

Wanting more stuff is not a new postmodern problem. But the dilemma in our culture is that we don't keep up just with the Joneses; we're trying to keep up with the affluence that's plastered all over our TVs. Try to imagine the frustration of a child living in poverty in the inner city and seeing the constant barrage of toy commercials on Saturday mornings. Is it any real surprise that teenagers with no strong moral authorities in their lives will mug someone for their Nikes? We have produced an entire generation of consumer-conscious kids.

I believe that nothing breaks the power of consumerism over us and our families faster than practicing generosity. It's the key to becoming outward focused. Recently I was washing windshields for free at a gas station with a family that had been coming to our church for only a month. They had quickly realized that generosity—as expressed in serving others—was a natural part of Christianity, and they wanted to experience it.

Just think what could happen if God helped us tear down this idol of consumerism in our lives. Just think what our churches might look like . . . what our city might become. What if it became the norm that the most natural thing for a new Christian to do was serve others?

Are you ready for this? Here's one of the most common questions I get as a pastor: "Should I tithe on my gross or my net income?"

After years of hearing this, I want to say, "You've got to be kidding." But of course I don't.

Sometimes it takes a long time for a perspective to change. It really isn't about gross or net. It's not even about tithing. It's about unbridled generosity.

Let me stretch it further. Generosity is not limited by what you don't have. When you think you don't have anything to give, that you're strapped for money, that things couldn't be any tighter for you, then refer to this amazing account Paul gives of some Christians in Greece:

> Now, friends, I want to report on the surprising and generous ways in which God is working in the churches in Macedonia province. Fierce troubles came down on the people of those churches, pushing them to the very limit. The trial exposed their true colors: They were incredibly happy, though desperately poor. The pressure triggered something totally unexpected: an outpouring of pure and generous gifts. I was there and saw it for myself. They gave offerings of whatever they could—far more than they could afford!—pleading for the privilege of helping out in the relief of poor Christians.
>
> 2 Corinthians 8:1–4 Message

Sometime back I got a letter from a single mom. After a devastating divorce that left her broken, she wrote about hearing me speak one weekend on being outward focused. Her letter read:

> I began to wonder just why I come every week. I come, I figured, because it refreshed me and got me ready to face another week. But that was not what this church was all about. I was truly inward focused, and now I was being called on it. The question was, what was I going to do about it? . . .

After we got home that night we tried to figure out what God wanted us to do. It didn't take long. I felt a strong desire to do a Christmas outreach to the projects in Hamilton. . . . So we started buying things: toys, blankets, food, baby items, household cleaners, hats, gloves, underwear, socks, and more. . . . On Christmas Eve, we parked the van on the street and lifted the back, and in three minutes there was a mob of people around asking about the stuff. We told them that it was free. We had never in our lives experienced the love of God like this before. To see children put on a pair of gloves or a hat or even slippers and watch their faces light up was a life-changing moment for us, and we have not been the same since. Two weeks later we were back with more. . . . I felt like the reformed Grinch in that "my heart grew three sizes that day!" I had found true peace and love and joy.

We are going again in February with Valentine treats for the kids. In April we will be taking Easter baskets and umbrellas. In June we're going to have a "Summer Blowout" and buy 100 burgers from McDonald's for a picnic. In August we will be bringing backpacks with school supplies. In October we'll take candy for parents to pass out to neighborhood children. Then we're back to December to start it all over again. We have heard [God] calling and have responded. We couldn't have done it without this wonderful, wacky place we call our church. And now we no longer just attend, we serve!

One side note: after the divorce, we were forced to sell our home. The children had to sell most of their treasures. We had nowhere to live and no money. I had been a stay-at-home mom for twenty years. . . . We were lost. We moved into my parents' basement. . . . There are no doors down there; there is even less privacy. My son doesn't have a bed to sleep on; he uses the couch. I felt like a failure. The kids never really complained, but I knew they felt cheated. They missed their rooms and their stuff and their old life.

But then something happened—we saw what poor really was. We were never hungry. We were always warm. We had furniture. And we had each other and a loving God who has never let us down, and you know what? All of a sudden that basement seemed like Buckingham Palace!

Thank you, Ronda Rubio

About one hundred years after Jesus was crucified, the Christian philosopher Aristides wrote, "If there is among [the Christians] a man that is poor and needy, and they have not an abundance of necessaries, they fast two or three days that they may supply the needy with their necessary food."[3]

Wow. We've got to break out of the 10 percent thing. I can't believe that I ever complained about tithing, about giving a percentage to the church. Especially when I read the extent to which the early Christians went to express the love of Jesus. We are living in a dream world of self-focused insanity. If we want real life, we've got to let go of the crazy one we're holding on to.

Some people from the Vineyard go out every Saturday morning—rain, sleet, snow, or hail—to Washington Park downtown to hand out bologna sandwiches. But the real reason is to build relationships with folks who are in a tough spot. Washington Park has been ground zero for a number of the homeless in downtown Cincinnati for years.

One day one of these servants sent me an amazing email:

Two years ago, while passing out bologna sandwiches in Washington Park, I met a homeless man named Mario. He literally had only the clothes on his back. Mario and I became . . . friends, and I began sharing stories with him about how Jesus had turned my life around, and . . . I finally had peace in my heart. Six months after I met Mario, we were sitting on the steps of the gazebo in Washington Park, and he turned to me and said, "I want that peace," so I prayed with him. We cried and hugged each other, and I could see that there was now hope in his eyes. He struggled with his addiction but became faithful in trusting the Lord and reading his Word.

After being clean for a year from drugs, Mario now had a job at one of the local hotels, an apartment, and a life that he was living for God. One day he told me that he had his daughter's three little girls (ages three, five, and seven) living with him. Their mother was addicted to crack and hadn't been taking care of them. He asked me if I could give him some extra bologna sandwiches for the girls' lunches through the week to help out. It became a weekly routine: he would show up at the park on Saturday mornings, and I would give him a bag of extra bologna sandwiches, potato chips, and fruit for the girls.

Five months later Mario came up to me and said that he had something for me. He explained to me that the girls did not have many toys but that they wanted to give "something special" to the lady that gives Grandpa "the extra bologna sandwiches." He handed me a very worn-out teddy bear. He said, "I know it's not much, but . . . they wanted me to make sure that I give this to you and tell you thanks."

It's all about perspective. And heart.

I have to remind myself on a regular basis that "small things done with great love will change the world." We have that mission statement engraved on our building. But I still forget it. Often.

A woman came up to me after one of our celebrations and wanted to talk. I knew she was a single mom with a couple of kids and a lot on her shoulders. She lived on very little. She wrestled with bipolar disorder. Life had not been simple or easy. But she began to tell me how serving had changed her life over the years. Dramatically.

For Christmas someone had given her a gift coupon book from Taco Bell. She went to the drive-through to grab dinner for herself and her kids. After she gave the cashier her coupons, she noticed in the mirror that the person in the car behind her seemed to be frantically looking for change in the seat. She said to the cashier, "How much is the bill for the car behind me?" The guy told her, and she said, "Is there enough in the coupon book to cover it?" He thumbed through the pages and said, "Yeah, this will just cover it." She said, "Keep it. And tell the person that God loves them." The cashier gave her a dumbfounded look, smiled, and said, "Okay." And with that, she drove off.

She told me how grateful she felt that someone had given her those coupons in the first place and that God had allowed her to see an opportunity to serve—and how real his presence seemed to be the moment she drove away.

One day Jesus was sitting in the temple, observing as people put money in the offering. When a widow placed two small coins in the collection, he smiled at his disciples and said, "Did you see that? She just gave more than all the other people combined. She gave out of her need." (See Mark 12:41–44.)

We have very poor ways of measuring what is valuable, what is generous, what is kind, what is sacrifice. That's why we're not God. I have a feeling that what my friend did with her coupon book was a big deal to the Father. A small thing done with great love.

One day Jesus told an odd story after encountering a young man having a difficult time deciding if he was going to follow Jesus:

> God's kingdom is like a factory owner who hired some guys early in the morning for his factory. They agreed on eighty dollars a day and went to work. Later the owner found more men hanging out in the city, unemployed. He told them to go to his factory and he'd pay them a fair wage. Off they went. The same thing happened at noon and again at three o'clock. Even at five he found some guys loitering. "Why are you just standing around?" he asked.
>
> "Because no one hired us," they said.
>
> The owner said, "Go to my factory. I'll give you work."
>
> When the day ended, the owner said to the foreman, "Call in all the workers and give them their wages. Start with the last hired." Those hired at five o'clock got eighty dollars. The ones who started at eight were furious. They said, "Hey, these guys only worked for an hour. We were sweating for nine long hours, and you paid them what we made."
>
> The owner said, "Friends, didn't we agree on your wage? I haven't been unfair to you. If I want to be generous with my money, can't I do what I want? Are you envious because I am generous?"
>
> Matthew 20:1–15, author's paraphrase

In the Greek, Jesus is literally saying, "Is your eye evil [envious] because I'm good [generous]?" In other words, how you see the problem may be the problem.

For the factory workers, this was an issue of fairness. But their problem really was the generosity of the manager—and an internalized issue with envy. Healthy spiritual eyesight is critical, isn't it? As Jesus put it, how can you take the splinter out of your co-worker's eye when you've got a log in your own (see Matt. 7:4)? Serving lost people—who we might think deep down don't deserve our service—doesn't always make sense or seem fair.

But maybe that's not the real problem. Maybe it's our eyesight.

A friend of mine in another church began doing outward-focused, free giveaways with some buddies, and they had the most fun with one they affectionately called the "45-second grab-away." One day they passed out leaflets in a housing area, letting people know when they would be back to pass out free pencil cases filled with pens, pencils, and rulers they had purchased for kids going back to school. When they returned, they were met by a mob of over one hundred kids. There was no sense in trying to form a line; they were mobbed and gave away sixty pencil cases in less than one minute—no kidding!

When they saw little kids with tears and disappointed faces because they didn't get one, they pulled out some of their church's connect cards and quickly wrote "Good for one free case" on them. They told the kids they'd be back on Friday. The group of friends walked away excited but unsure of how they could afford to buy another sixty pencil cases. They headed off to an office supply store. When the manager asked them why they were buying so many pencil cases and heard their story, he said, "You buy the cases, and I'll fill them for free!" Shortly afterward, my friend got an unexpected gift that covered the cost of the extra cases, and he was once again amazed at how God supplies our need—in order to give away!

One of the guys on my friend's team said, "If you had told me two months ago that we would be seeing things like this happening, and that God would be using us to do this kind of stuff, I'd have said you were mad. I just can't believe it, but I can't wait to find out what God has planned next. I've never personally experienced God like this before!"

How fun—and how simple—is that? And even though it stretched the group a little bit financially, isn't it amazing how God provides when we begin to step outside ourselves? What a small thing, giving pencils and pens. But to be able to express God's kindness and generosity in such a tangible and practical way? Priceless.

In doing any ministry that is geared toward serving and giving away resources, some people get concerned that they might get ripped off. Many times I've been asked, "Don't you worry that some people will take advantage of what you're doing?" I respond, "No, I'm not worried. I know they will!" I think the stats are pretty good that we'll get ripped off. As a matter of fact, I think that's a scriptural idea.

When Jesus told the story of the farmer planting seeds in Mark 4, there was an extravagance in how the farmer flung the seeds. They weren't carefully placed in predug holes, one at a time, in tight, precisely measured rows. There seemed to be a happy abandonment and not a scarcity mentality at all: the more seed thrown, the better the chances of harvest. But the return didn't seem that great. I'm no statistician and can barely do simple math, but it looks like only one in four seeds did anything. But wow—the ones that did produced crops of thirty, sixty, or even a hundred times what was sown! Many of us would feel ripped off with only a 25 percent success rate.

I'd like a bumper sticker that says, "Love 'em all . . . and let God sort 'em out." Isn't that risky? Probably, but only because real love is vulnerable. I love this famous quote from C. S. Lewis:

> To love at all is to be vulnerable. Love anything, and your heart will certainly be wrung and possibly be broken. If you want to make sure of keeping it intact, you must give your heart to no one, not even to an animal. Wrap it carefully round with hobbies and little luxuries; avoid all entanglements; lock it up safe in the casket or coffin of your selfishness. But in that casket—safe, dark, motionless, airless—it will change. It will not be broken; it will become unbreakable, impenetrable, irredeemable. . . . The only place outside Heaven where you can be perfectly safe from all the dangers of love is Hell.[4]

Let's be seed flingers, thrusting our hands into God's abundant supply of mercy and grace and flinging it everywhere. And let's all agree we'll get taken advantage of from time to time.

Jesus said, "The thief comes only to steal and kill, and destroy; I came that they may have life, and have it abundantly" (John 10:10 NASB).

The abundant life. Living large. That's what Jesus offers.

Years ago when our girls were in elementary school, some friends of ours knew we needed a break and offered to let us stay in a little house they had just built way out in the country, near Hillsboro, Ohio. They had bought about a hundred acres and just wanted a place their family could go to in the hills to relax. Our friends were fairly wealthy, so we were thinking this place might be a cool little cabin. When we got there, we realized the house must have cost over half a million dollars, which was really a lot back then. There were black walnut wood floors (including the laundry room), a digital TV, four bedrooms, a huge stone fireplace—state-of-the-art everything. We were in shock. A huge warehouse over the hill housed trucks, QuadRunners, BMX bikes, WaveRunners for a lake they were putting in, security alarm systems, and a guest room above the warehouse.

But that's not what I mean by living large.

Here's living large: around midnight we all went out in our pajamas, lay on the driveway, and stared at the sky full of millions of stars with no city lights nearby to diffuse them. Every few minutes we would see a shooting star and scream, "Did you see that?" We were serenaded by the crickets as we lay on the cool summer asphalt. Yet none of it was ours. The only thing that belonged to me was the love of my wife and two little girls, and a used car that ran most of the time . . . but I felt like the richest man on the planet, watching a light show that God provided. That's living large.

Nothing is ours to keep. It's all God's.

One day on an outreach, I gave a bag of groceries to an older woman living alone in a dark, claustrophobic apartment in the projects. I asked her if she had anything—anything at all—that I could pray for her about. She took my hand, smiled, and said,

"My arthritis is acting up. I would just like to be able to get to my church tomorrow." And for the thousandth time in my life, I took a calculated risk and prayed a dangerous prayer: *Come, Holy Spirit, come.*

So we prayed together, and she and I experienced the abundant life of God.

Here's one difference between *religion* and *relationship with Jesus*: religion can be calculated and measured; Jesus is extravagant.

Most of us know the story of the Good Samaritan, the guy who helped a man who had been mugged and was passed over by the religious folks. If we could really get the context of the parable, we would see that it was told to humorously shock Jesus's audience and stretch his listeners.

The Samaritans were the despised half-breed race in Israel, the people who didn't have correct theology and didn't even worship in the right place. Yet the Samaritan becomes the focal point of what extravagant mercy looks like. The two coins the Samaritan gave the hotel manager were each equivalent to a day's wages, so if he was netting $400 a week, those coins equaled $160, and he promised to reimburse any further costs.

Earlier, Jesus had told the people to do good to their enemies, that God was kind even to ungrateful and cranky people. Like those who cut in line in front of us. Or who won't let us in on the expressway ramp. Or who pull into a parking space just before we do.

Another time, Jesus said something that I think is terrifying: "If you do not forgive men their sins, your Father will not forgive your sins" (Matt. 6:15). At one level that sounds so petty, so conditional. Is that how God is? But our refusal to forgive exposes a fracture in our souls—that at some point deep down we really don't believe that God has forgiven us. There is a divine psychology at work here. We cannot receive what we will not give away.

Author and psychiatrist Karl Menninger once said, "Generous people are rarely mentally ill."[5] Try some spontaneous giving of mercy. Toward someone close to you, someone at work, or someone who is probably in need of a little bit of mercy. Don't be stingy with your giving; it may reveal how much you really believe you have been forgiven. I think the beauty of trying a few simple, outward-focused acts is that they reflect God's abundant generosity.

Generous people think in terms of abundance, rarely scarcity. There's an interesting story of this slant in Genesis. Abram and his nephew Lot had prospered in terms of cattle, sheep, and goats, but the land couldn't support them both. After a while some of the workers and relatives were fighting with each other over land, water wells, and so on. This could have been a time for Abram to argue about rights and who was the patriarch, but he had grown in his trust of God's ability to provide. His abundance mentality enabled him to view problems with a win-win approach: "Abram talked it over with Lot. 'This arguing between our herdsmen has got to stop,' he said. 'After all, we are close relatives! I'll tell you what we'll do. Take your choice of any section of the land you want, and we will separate. If you want that area over there, then I'll stay here. If you want to stay in this area, then I'll move on to another place'" (Gen. 13:8–9).

There's a simple way to develop that kind of abundance mentality. Let me give you an example from a physical perspective: if you work out, is it because you want to be around to take care of the people you love—perhaps the best insurance you can buy— or because you want to be a chick magnet? That's the difference between having an inward focus or an outward focus.

In my case, when my worldview has mostly me in the center of it, something begins to get out of whack. And one of the ways I can determine how much of my life is in the center is how I allocate my resources: my emotions, my thoughts, my money, my time. How much is focused on me? Left to my own devices, I find that I can be a very selfish man. So I have to learn to think differently.

Now here's the real dilemma: if you have an inward focus, the most you have in your reserves is what you're capable of producing, because you're focused on yourself. People with an inward focus typically live with a scarcity view of life.

We had a young woman named Joie in our church who really caught hold of being outward focused. She attended a university in Florida, and for spring break she decided to go on a servant evangelism road trip with a couple of girlfriends. She bought 150 bottles of water with a special label printed on them: "Jesus said, 'Everyone who drinks this water will be thirsty again, but whoever drinks the water I give him will never thirst.'"

She sent us a "Road Rules" email:

> In Ocala . . . we met up with a friend of ours who was putting us up for the night. We had the opportunity to meet her church college ministry group and tell them about what we were trying to do.
>
> They were amazed. One guy, who was a missionary in the Philippines for four years, called us revolutionaries! He was doing a series on "Ways to Share Our Faith" with the college group. It just so happened that his message the next week came from the same verse on our water bottles. If nothing else, we've planted a seed in Ocala.
>
> In Mobile, Alabama, . . . we handed out the bottles of water outside a Burlington Coat Factory. In Jacksonville we hooked up with a local church plant. I called the pastor and found out that a couple who had been members of the church for about two weeks were in an unfortunate situation and needed help moving.
>
> So, Friday we moved the remainder of their belongings. Due to past experiences with previous churches and Christians, they were skeptical about relying on the kindness of strangers. They said they didn't know that people like us still existed—people willing to do hard-core manual labor for perfect strangers just because we wanted to share God's love. It was just really awesome to serve them in their time of need and to see how truly thankful they were. God's plans rock!

How cool is that? While other college students were bingeing on the beaches, these revolutionaries found a whole new way to party. It makes this old guy want to do a free car wash in a toga.

Attitude

Paul's short letter to the Philippian church underscored his belief that developing a servant attitude is critical for fulfillment and joy. He wrote, "Your attitude should be the same that Christ Jesus had. Though he was God, he did not demand and cling to his rights as God. He made himself nothing; he took the humble position of a slave and appeared in human form" (Phil. 2:5–7 NLT).

Did you catch the word *attitude*? Attitude is our feeling about something. It's our mental position about life, how we see it and react. Airplane pilots use the term *attitude* to describe the horizontal relationship the plane has with the ground. Pilots have an attitude indicator that shows if the nose of the plane is up or down. In general, if the nose is up, the plane will soar upward; if the nose is down, the plane will eventually have a date with the dirt. Attitude is critical in a plane—it affects altitude, how high the plane can soar. It's the same thing for us humans.

Our attitude is the one thing we can change. Think about it: you can't change the way people act, you can't change your past, you can't change the gifts you have or don't have, you can't change the circumstances that slime you. But attitude probably has more to do with the direction of your life—something you can change—than success or failure.

Paul's attitude about life was formed not by his past (he had Christians put to death), not by his abilities (he said that people found him pretty unimpressive in person), not by his circumstances (he was in prison), and not by moral credentials (he said he was the worst of all sinners).

Paul wanted the saints in Philippi to understand that "God is working in you, giving you the desire to obey him and the power to do what pleases him" (Phil. 2:13 NLT). In other words, God himself is living inside you to work out your life in such a way that it fulfills his goals for the universe. For Paul, servanthood was a liberating lifestyle of purpose.

Our attitude shapes the way we think about serving others, and servanthood is the attitude critical for personal fulfillment.

Have you ever really thought about happiness? Perhaps most of us have only a vague idea of what it is, and it's usually defined by a future state. We'd be happy if things would settle down in our lives, if we had only half of the people mad at us that are currently mad at us, if we had a spouse, if we had a different spouse, if we were married to George Clooney or Halle Berry, if we had a car other than a Dodge Dart Swinger, if we had a certain level of income, if we had less turmoil in our lives, if we had . . . (fill in the blank).

Author and counselor Chris Thurman writes about a teenage client who was obsessive about things having to go a certain way for him to have a good day. Thurman asked him to make a list of what would have to happen for a day to be a good one. His list included:

waking up to a favorite song playing on the clock radio,
wearing a specific set of clothes and tennis shoes,
not having to eat oatmeal, scrambled eggs, or bran cereal,
getting the front seat on the school bus,
all his friends saying nice things to him all day long.

The list went on for so long and was so detailed that it was impossible for everything to go as he wanted. Consequently, he'd never had a happy day. Something always spoiled it.

I wonder if most of us have a little of that attitude in us. Be honest: are you the type who can't enjoy a movie if someone sits in front of you or can't enjoy a meal if the service is slow?

In 1 Thessalonians 5, Paul wrote, "Be joyful always; pray continually; give thanks in all circumstances, for this is God's will for you in Christ Jesus" (vv. 16–18). That's not an exercise in futility; it takes us from an inward focus regarding how we want things to an outward focus on the God to whom we are surrendered. Outwardness is a discipline we have to exercise. Jesus said it makes us way happier to give than to receive. Maybe serving others is one way to jump-start happiness in our lives.

Suppose you woke up one day after being blind all of your life and suddenly you could see. In her book *Pilgrim at Tinker Creek*, Annie Dillard recounts stories from surgeons who discovered how to perform safe cataract operations. Hundreds of people who had been blind since birth because of cataracts could see for the first time. The surgeons told of the confusion their patients had with concepts such as space and depth. Things as simple as shadows were terrifically unnerving. One father was dejected to find his twenty-one-year-old daughter shutting her eyes to walk around the house, especially on the stairs. Her doctor wrote, "She is never happier or more at ease than when, by closing her eyelids, she relapses into her former state of total blindness."[1]

Some patients embraced their new sight. One was astonished by his own hands, bending and stretching them endlessly. Another was overcome by the brightness and kept her eyes shut for two weeks. When she finally opened them, she didn't recognize any objects but gazed with astonishment at everything, saying over and over, "Oh, God! How beautiful!" A little girl was taken outside to a garden and stood speechless in front of a tree, not knowing what it was until she touched it, and then called it "the tree with the lights in it."[2]

Wouldn't it be amazing if we could really see God's power and beauty? They cannot be seen with our world-worn eyes. We have spiritual cataracts that fog our vision. Wouldn't it be awesome if we could look at God with fresh eyes and be astonished once again, as if we were seeing for the first time "the tree with the lights in it"?

I think we get a glimpse of that when we begin to understand that the kingdom is made up of servants, and only those who serve can begin to see it. It was Milton's devil in *Paradise Lost* who said, "Better to reign in Hell than to serve in Heaven." There is something liberating, something pure, about serving others with no strings attached.

As Jesus put it, "Blessed are the pure in heart, for they will see God" (Matt. 5:8).

In his *New York Times* bestselling book *Duty*, author Bob Greene told about returning to Columbus, Ohio, to be with his dying father. After his dad died, Greene connected with an eighty-four-year-old man in Columbus who could be one of any anonymous old men drinking coffee. But this man was Paul Tibbets, a World War II pilot who survived twenty-five missions over Europe. It was at age twenty-nine that Tibbets flew the harrowing mission over Japan in a B-29 that dropped the first atomic bomb.

Greene spent many afternoons asking Paul Tibbets questions about the World War II generation, trying to make sense out of the emotional distance he had felt between himself and his deceased father, who had received a Bronze Star for leading platoons of infantrymen through hellish warfare in France and Italy.

In one conversation with Tibbets, in which Greene wondered if the war years were the best years of his dad's life, Tibbets said, "Could be. . . . [Your dad] was very satisfied with what he was doing. He told himself that he was in the war for his family and for his country, and he was surrounded by men who were telling themselves the same thing. It wasn't comfortable and it wasn't fun, but there was never a day when you thought that what you were doing didn't matter."[3]

Those words jumped off the page at me. That's what I long for. Immediately I thought, *Do I live my life in such a way that there is never a day when I think that what I'm doing doesn't matter?* Without getting dramatic, I have to remind myself every so often that we are engaged in a great spiritual war for the souls of men and women. *God, keep me outwardly focused.*

When Jesus washed the feet of his disciples, including the one who would betray him, he said he was giving us an example of how we were to live. What's more, he said in John 13:17, "Now that you know these things, you will be blessed if you do them."

What if there were never days when we thought that what we were doing didn't matter? There never are, when we become servants of God.

Each year we host an event called SOS—Summer of Service— where teenagers from different churches all over the Midwest spend a week with us. We hold Bible studies in the mornings and train them on becoming servants, offer subwoofer-pumped worship each night, and take them out each afternoon to serve others in practical ways.

Last year we had twenty-five school buses carry kids all over the city. By the end of the week, several of the bus drivers began joining the outreaches. One team went door-to-door planting flowers. An elderly woman told them she had just been praying for someone to help with her garden because the doctor said she couldn't work in it due to health problems. She was thrilled!

One student had the same person ask him five times what he was really doing the outreach for—what the hidden meaning was behind "showing God's love in a practical way." In another part of town, a city council member thanked the group for changing the neighborhood . . . and asked if they would please come back.

We sent one group to a day camp in the city to spend time hanging out with kids. By the end of the week, the camp kids had become so attached to the SOS students that they cried when they found out the students wouldn't be coming back the next week.

In only one neighborhood did we have a little problem. Students were passing out free water bottles at an intersection when the police pulled up, asked them where they were from, and told them they weren't allowed to solicit. They said, "We're not soliciting. This is free!" The police told them they couldn't preach. They said, "We're not preaching, we're just serving!" The students were asked to leave and not come back. So they left. The next day they went to the police station and gave the police bags of goodies and thanked them for serving their community.

Think of the lesson these kids learned in how to respond in Jesus-led, servant ways instead of reacting negatively. Some of us jaded adults could learn something there.

I have a theory: I think developing an outward focus to life will do more for inward transformation than perhaps anything else.

I bet I've read the passage of Luke 12:6, 13–15 hundreds of times, but I've never connected the second part of it until recently. First Jesus gave a great illustration of the Father heart of God: "Are not five sparrows sold for two pennies? Yet not one of them is forgotten by God. Indeed, the very hairs of your head are all numbered. Don't be afraid; you are worth more than many sparrows" (v. 6). Then, only a few verses later in this sermon, someone yelled to Jesus from the audience: "'Teacher, tell my brother to divide the inheritance with me.' Jesus replied, 'Man, who appointed me a judge or an arbiter between you?' Then he said to them, 'Watch out! Be on your guard against all kinds of greed; a man's life does not consist in the abundance of his possessions'" (vv. 13–15).

Do you see the connection between those two passages? Jesus did some on-the-fly, divine psychoanalysis on that dude. I bet that was the last question the guy ever asked in a crowd with Jesus around.

First, Jesus implied that God doesn't exist primarily to judge between people, in this case two people. He is here to judge between us and himself. The issue wasn't between this guy and his crooked brother; it was between this guy and his God. You see how sneaky we can be in trying to manipulate God?

Second, this man was concerned about his future in a way that apparently raised a red flag for Jesus. The man was saying there should be fairness in what was coming to him. But Jesus was concerned about his character and his lack of trust in God as his provider. That's what he had just been teaching on, and this guy didn't get it. And so Jesus said, "Watch out!"

The pressure to turn inward and worry or demand our rights from God is powerful. It must be some of the residue of a fallen nature that clings to us like the seaweed that probably hung on Jonah after God corrected his course.

This email was a turnaround: the server got served.

Dear Dave,

After hearing you tell a story about a woman who scraped her last bit of change from the couch to buy her child a meal at McDonald's, only to find that her food had been paid for by the car in front of her at the drive-through window, I was moved and started sharing the Lord's love in a similar way. From time to time, I buy the food for the car behind me at fast-food drive-throughs. Each time I do, it's started a conversation among my children about giving to others. Just this morning, I had a chance to experience firsthand what it was like to be on the receiving end.

I went to the Starbucks near our school to buy a coffee for myself and one to surprise my daughter's teacher. I was next in line to order when the gentleman in front of me turned and asked, "What are you getting?" I told him my choices and then he turned to the cashier and said he was going to pay for mine too. I smiled, remembering your story about the McDonald's, and knowing I had enough money to pay myself, I said, "Thank you, but you needn't do that." He told me he wanted to share God's love. At that moment a warm feeling ran through my body from top to bottom, as I knew that God was with me. It was a reminder that he is there even when things are going well.

Every sip of that coffee this morning reminded me that I am not alone. Later on in the day, I reflected back on this encounter and realized even more. My husband died two years ago of cancer, and Monday was to be our twenty-fourth wedding anniversary. I am not angry, just feeling sad and a bit lonely.

Today's experience of kindness opened my eyes; I realized that I am loved! I will not only remember God's love, I will feel his warm hug throughout my body with every sip of hot coffee I take.

In his name, Judy

Is God's timing good or what?

I read a psychological study that supposedly showed that human beings have sixty thousand thoughts a day. Assuming we think when we're sleeping, that's about forty-two thoughts per minute, which is dangerously close to a thought per second. I don't know; that sounds like a lot of thinking. I'm not sure I believe that. On the other hand, try not thinking anything for the next five seconds.

It made me wonder, though: how many of those thoughts are about myself?

I thought about myself—how often do I think about myself? Even that thought was wacky—I thought about myself about how often I think about myself. I think I think about myself a lot. I wonder what people think about me. Or I pass by a window and look at my reflection. I told my wife the other day that I thought there was something really wrong with me, that as I'm getting older, my head is actually getting smaller and I look like a big tick. She said, "Honey, it's not your head. You need to go on a diet." Or I'm in a conversation and I'm wondering about how I'm coming off. *Do I sound stupid? Am I being a good pastor?* I drive my car thinking about how late I am for my next meeting. Or if I'm really spiritual, I'm thinking about how unspiritual I really am. It's all about me.

There's a lot going on in my brain about me. And whether it's positive or negative, a lot of my thinking is about myself. Can you relate to this at all, or is it just me? See? Now I'm thinking about myself wondering if I'm the only one who thinks about himself a lot.

This isn't good, especially when the Bible says not to worry about our lives, to deny ourselves, or, as Paul writes, to "take captive every thought to make it obedient to Christ" (2 Cor. 10:5).

Be careful of being hyper-introspective; that can become an inward-focused vortex. Just cut it short and make a difference in someone else's life—go serve them.

et me give you a radical outward-focused thought: we were made for God's pleasure and purposes, not for ours. Right away that causes a problem for most of us. And here's the best analogy I can think of—dogs and cats.

I'm a dog kind of guy. When I'd come home from elementary school, my dog would jump up, tail wagging, mouth open and panting, and ready to play, as if to say, "Where have you been all day?"

After I grew up and moved away from home, somehow I inherited a cat. Cats are very different animals. When I'd come home from work, the cat would just look at me like, "Finally, the help has arrived." He'd give you that "What's in this for me?" look. Dogs have owners; cats have a staff. I know there are cat people and there are dog people, but I don't understand you cat people. You're a persistent bunch. But as comedian Jeff Valdez says, "Cats are smarter than dogs. You can't get eight cats to pull a sled through snow." Maybe there's something to that.

But dogs seem to understand that they were created for their master's pleasure and for his purposes. I tend to think of humankind as a huge herd of cats on God's forty acres. We must be a mess to manage.

In his mind-bending vision, John the apostle writes in Revelation that a group of people around the throne of God would periodically fall down in overpowering awe and reverence and say, "You are worthy, O Lord our God, to receive glory and honor and power. For you created everything, and it is for your pleasure that they exist and were created" (Rev. 4:11 NLT).

The Bible is very clear on this—and frankly, I think most of us are a little uncomfortable with it—that we exist for God's pleasure, God's purposes, not ours. That's why he made us. That's pretty humbling when you think about it.

How about this for an outward-focused topic: hell. Sometimes people will ask me how I could believe in a God who would send someone to hell. And sometimes in a moment of honesty I'll say I don't know. It's hard for me to grasp all of that as well.

But I'll follow it up with this: if we cannot conceive of a God who could send someone to hell, what does that say about that same God who would hand his own Son over to a tortuous death to rescue us from that end? The story is this: our condition is so heinous, so unapproachable, so hideous, that only the drastic measure of a perfect sacrifice could drive the disease of sin from us. The Bible says that God has no delight in the punishment of the wicked. The entire race is infected with an AIDS-like virus that destroys the soul—and only one antidote exists.

Sin so miniaturizes the human condition that the first step into God's presence is as high as Mount Everest. We cannot step up; we are unable to. That puts hell in another perspective for me. God, who must separate the infected from the healthy, comes to us with the vaccine drawn from his own veins. The looming of hell makes the love of God even greater. Hell is the only refuge from a holy, perfect love.

Do I believe in a literal hell? In some ways, what difference does it make? A dream is just as terrifying if one never wakes up. If the images of fire, worms, and thirst that Jesus used were metaphorical, then I would prefer those to the awful reality he is trying to convey.

But one of the most remarkable outward-focused thoughts about hell was written by Paul the apostle in Romans: "I wish I could help my Jewish brothers and sisters, my people. I would even wish that I were cursed and cut off from Christ if that would help them" (Rom. 9:3 NCV).

That's stunning. Even if I could understand eternity more clearly, I honestly don't think I'd say I would suffer hell to bring people closer to God. Now, that's an outward focus.

In the decades of doing outreaches, I've probably gone into hundreds of people's homes to pray for them while bringing a bag of groceries. I can't tell you how many times I've walked into a dark room in the projects, with the curtains pulled and little kids with powdered doughnuts sitting in front of a TV blasting Saturday cartoons, and saying to a parent, "Would you like prayer for anything?" They usually respond, somewhat surprised, with something like, "My husband's in jail" or "I need a job" or "I've been really sick" or whatever. Have you ever tried to pray while *Bratz* is blaring in the background? It's hard. It's distracting. It's tough to hear what God is saying.

Satan's temptation of Jesus was designed to distract him from hearing his Father's voice and divert him from his mission. Jesus came to roll out the kingdom of God, to defeat the enemy, and to set men and women free.

So let me ask you a personal question: why would Satan tempt little ol' you? You get up and go to work or school or fight with rugrats every day. You don't hurt anyone; you're just a regular Joe or Josephine trying to do the right thing. Why would the enemy bother you? Because Jesus said in John 20:21, "As the Father has sent me, I am sending you." In other words, you have the same mission Jesus had. Of course, the enemy wants to distract you from hearing your Father's voice and to divert you from what your true mission is in life. As Oswald Chambers put it, Satan "does not come to us on the premise of tempting us to sin, but on the premise of shifting our point of view, and only the Spirit of God can detect this as a temptation of the devil."[4]

This isn't about you just having an affair or just looking at one more porn site or just thinking about someone else as your husband or just cheating a little bit on your test. This is way larger than your personal sins; Jesus can forgive those and clean you up. This is about distraction and diversion from your true destiny and calling and mission.

What if serving others was our true destiny? What if, like Jesus, we said that we didn't come to be served, but rather to serve others? How would that change how we respond to temptation?

In the book *Under the Overpass*, two Christian college students spent about half a year in five different cities, living with the homeless—eating and sleeping in dumpsters, exhausted, in danger, hungry, depressed, and cold. After the experience, they came away with this idea: "Only in knowing God will we see people as they are." Author Mike Yankoski writes:

> The "love your neighbor" part of Jesus' teaching starts with the simple actions and small opportunities that are available to each of us. Little things do mean a lot, especially in the kingdom of God, where giving a drink of cold water has eternal repercussions. And I am convinced that the more committed we become to impacting one person at a time—whether through a cup of coffee or a genuine conversation—the more we'll prepare our hearts and our churches to respond at both a community and national level. The bottom line is that real love always shows itself in action.[5]

That sounds a little like the idea that small things done with great love will change the world. It's not that we don't need to tackle the big systemic issues of racism, social justice, or economic inequities. We do. But life is rarely either/or. We also need to begin with a personal touch; otherwise it becomes more about a cause than love.

Listen how simple God makes this. In Isaiah 58:7 he says, "I want you to share your food with the hungry and to welcome poor wanderers into your homes. Give clothes to those who need them, and do not hide from relatives who need your help."

Part of my problem for years was that I was afraid of the poor—afraid I wouldn't say the right thing, afraid they would be really different from me, afraid I wouldn't know what to do, afraid I might get sucked into a black hole of time and energy, afraid I might get ripped off.

With the life transformation God has in mind for each of us—he longs to give us real life, real meaning, real purpose—maybe we need the poor more than they need us.

A few years ago an obstetrics nurse named Julie Armas and her husband, Alex, discovered during her pregnancy that her unborn baby had spina bifida, a condition in which the spinal cord is exposed, causing serious brain damage. From the Internet Julie discovered a surgeon, Joseph Bruner of the Vanderbilt University Medical Center, who was pioneering delicate surgeries while the fetus was still in the womb. Julie and Alex prayed and decided to go ahead with this radical new surgery, which was done with specially created miniature instruments with sutures thinner than a human hair. Everything would be performed through a tiny incision in the uterus, which would be carefully lifted outside the mother's body. A photographer was given permission to film the surgery, even though the fetus would never be seen.

With Julie only twenty-one weeks pregnant, the surgery took place. While Dr. Bruner was probing the incision, the unborn baby reached through the incision and grabbed on to the surgeon's finger—much to his chagrin. Dr. Bruner would periodically whisper to his staff during the surgery, "Shhh. You'll wake the baby." The photographer caught the photo, and it swirled around the Internet for months.

Five weeks later little Samuel Armas came screaming into the world, weighing in at a strapping five pounds eleven ounces. And now, years later, he is doing great and growing healthier every day, with no known brain damage. Julie said she and her husband wept for days when they later saw the photograph of little Samuel touching his healer.

I believe we are born with an innate need to touch something bigger than ourselves, something outside ourselves, to grasp the hand of our healer. To touch the hand that formed us.

The ultimate outward-focused thought is that something outside ourselves actually exists—a greater power, a personal God who longs for us to reach out to him. You can look for God inside yourself forever and not find him—at least not until you ask him in. But he's as near as the air itself. The first time you touch God's hand will be the moment you look for him outside yourself.

I think outward-focused people understand that this life is temporary. Solomon once wrote, "Naked a man comes from his mother's womb, and as he comes, so he departs. He takes nothing from his labor that he can carry in his hand" (Eccles. 5:15). In other words, we come in naked and we leave naked, so what's the best use of what we have?

This temporary world has a way of consuming our thoughts and energies. And with that myopic focus, we can lose the ability to see eternal strategies. We must learn to balance our feet in this world and our hearts in the next.

Leadership guru Warren Bennis recounts a story told to him by Liz Altman, a vice president at Motorola. Years earlier she was overwhelmed as she was working on her master's degree, finishing classes, interviewing for jobs, and doing a host of other things. She said:

> I spoke to a friend of mine who was about ten years older. I was explaining what was going on and she said, "So have you been snowboarding recently?" I kind of went ballistic. I said, "Snowboarding? Do you understand? Have you been listening to anything I've just said about what's going on in my life? I haven't written chapter two of my thesis yet and I have ten interviews and these people are all annoying me and I've got all these classes . . . and you're clearly not listening." She very quietly said, "Liz, you've never worked very well this way."
>
> Later I thought about it and decided to go snowboarding that weekend. . . . [As] corny as it sounds, I figured out the major issue of my thesis while I was snowboarding because I wasn't thinking about it at all. And literally halfway down the mountain I stopped and went, "You fool! Why aren't you thinking about it this way?"[6]

In the same way, some of us need to snowboard through eternity at times to help us solve problems in this world. There have been times when I've been worshiping or doing simple serving projects and had a major breakthrough in how to deal with a huge issue. Too much focus on this world throws us out of balance.

Each day quite a few cars cut through the Vineyard's parking lot to avoid traffic on the main roads. A staff member on our facilities team complained that these cars made it difficult to cut the grass, caused additional wear on our road, made it hazardous to cross on foot . . . blah blah blah. But one of his co-workers had a different perspective and suggested that instead of complaining about these people, we should serve them! So recently, he and the facilities team pulled out the grill and offered free hot dogs and drinks to everyone who cut through our parking lot that day. They stopped seeing the motorists as an annoyance and started seeing them as another opportunity to serve. Isn't that a classic paradigm shift? They went from complaining about too many cars cutting through to not having enough cars to serve!

Do you ever complain about people who annoy you? I do. Regularly.

Jesus's disciples were always complaining about people they found annoying. They tried to shoo away the kids who came to Jesus, ignore the blind man who wanted to be healed, hush the woman with a sick child, and basically protect Jesus from being bothered. But time and time again Jesus said, "Let the children alone, don't prevent them from coming to me. God's kingdom is made up of people like these" (Matt. 19:13 Message).

"People like these"—the blind, the sick, the young, the old, the broken. Look around you and identify the people you find annoying. At our church we sometimes use the term EGR, or Extra Grace Required, to remind us that God's grace extends to everyone, not just to our perfect selves. Maybe your EGR is a co-worker, or your mother-in-law, or a neighbor. Now think for a moment about how you can do something specifically to serve that person.

Perhaps you could start seeing that person as someone God loves and not just as someone who annoys you. And let's face it: you probably fit into someone else's "annoying person" category. How would you want to be treated?

On Christmas Eve, our church holds its annual doughnut outreach. Instead of a traditional Christmas Eve service, we meet at 4:00 p.m., sing a few Christmas carols, light candles, and pray . . . and then grab boxes of the twenty-four thousand Krispy Kreme doughnuts to give to people working that day. But one year, the Cincinnati weather was horrible: about ten degrees above zero with a foot of snow and ice that had dropped the day before. It seriously hurt our attendance. For the thousand or so people who came, though, it was a blast.

Later we got what I thought was going to be a negative email from someone who participated in this outreach. Everywhere she went—police stations and video stores and hotels—someone had beaten her there and had already given out doughnuts. She wrote:

> We were feeling irritated about our "wasted time." All of a sudden we saw an office building with a parking lot full of cars. The door was locked, but we decided to see if we could get a box to a security guard. A guard let us in. When we gave her the doughnuts and told her what we were doing, she started to cry. She couldn't believe we showed up when we did. Just moments before she was sitting alone, feeling sad, lonely, and completely forgotten. It turns out she had just moved to town, knew no one, and hadn't had any luck finding a church where she could "fit in." It's amazing how much power can be held in a box of doughnuts. A girl far from home at Christmas realized that she had not been forgotten by God or men, all because someone handed her a box of Krispy Kremes and reminded her that God loves her.
>
> She was getting ready to leave the lobby and go on her rounds when we showed up. Had we gotten there any earlier or later we would have missed her. She was still crying when we left, but she stopped long enough to ask, "Do you think I could go to that church?" She seemed very excited when we said, "Yeah, they take all kinds out there."

Who would have thought some doughnuts would open the door for a God conversation?

Grace

Developing an outward-focused approach to life begins with experiencing, then operating in, grace. Grace prevents us from thinking our performance enables us to enter into a healthy relationship with God. But the performance mentality so quickly creeps into our daily walk.

I deal with people in conflict all the time. Every week. And that's just the staff. The other day I had an epiphany and said to my wife, "Honey, you know what's wrong with the world? We're all really weird. Everybody. No one is exempt. And we don't even have a clue how weird we are. We are all so in need of grace."

One day Paul wrote to the Corinthian church, saying, "Hello, the clue phone's ringing—pick it up." The Message translation of 1 Corinthians 1:26–30 says:

> Take a good look, friends, at who you were when you got called into this life. I don't see many of "the brightest and the best" among you, not many influential, not many from high-society families. Isn't it obvious that God deliberately chose men and women that the culture overlooks and exploits and abuses, chose these "nobodies" to expose the hollow pretensions of the "somebodies"? That makes it quite clear that none of you can get by with blowing your own horn before God. Everything that we have—right thinking and right living, a clean slate and a fresh start—comes from God by way of Jesus Christ.

The moment we think we've gotten into this relationship with Jesus because we're more together than the bag lady in the West End, or we're a little sharper than the used car salesman with a comb-over that starts below his ear, or we have so much more to offer the kingdom of God than some poor slob who hasn't missed a single episode of *Jeopardy* since 1987, we're heading for trouble. We don't understand grace.

Serving people who don't know Jesus is the simplest way to refresh your grasp of grace. And don't forget: we're all really weird.

I magine the soundtrack from *Moulin Rouge* playing in the background and a voice saying, "There was a man who loved a woman deeply."

The woman was a prostitute. There may have been reams of reasons why she sold her body to men to do what they would. But her soul had shrunk to a size so small she could not hear it cry; she could hear only faint whimpers from time to time. But the man who loved this woman was mesmerized not by what she was but what she could be. Not by how she lived but how she could live. Not by the layers of makeup that now painted her worn face but by a beauty marred like a coin handled too many times, pocketed too much, and spent too easily.

He loved her. No, he was intoxicated by her. Why? Because he was married to her. He had married her when she was a prostitute. She had given him two sons and a daughter. Years later, when she had left him again, he traveled to the street corner where she sold herself each evening. Men knew who he was. They grinned and made jokes about his manhood. And in front of them all, he paid her pimp a sum of money to have her. The thugs in the alley laughed; what kind of husband had such little self-respect and so few prospects and was so pathetically romantic that he could not see what she was? But he knew exactly what she was. Though she was bathed in the mercury-vapor streetlight with her head hung in shame and her long curls hiding her eyes from his gaze, he knew deeply who she was. She was his wife. And these other men, these jackals, would never know her like that. Never. Because they had never known the glory of true love. So he took her home. Again.

Prophets sometimes had the tough job of serving as real-life dramatizations under the great director of this cosmic drama—God himself. And God was directing an autobiographical play—his love for his bride, Israel, which served as a microcosm of his love for the human race, his beautiful creation. The price he would pay to buy an unfaithful bride would be the life of his own Son.

The New Testament writer Paul said that all the events of the Old Testament served as allegories, as types. There was a hidden story between the lines.

I think we get the honor of having bit parts in this great drama. In serving lost people—even those whom we might consider undeserving—we get the privilege of expressing a mercy, a grace, a power that reflects the one who served us to his death.

It's the great story of the universe.

I magine you're a single mom. You've got a fifty-hour-a-week job and two kids. One kid is shuffled off to day care at 7:15 a.m., and the other catches a bus by herself. You worry about that every day. Yesterday you had a flat tire on the way home from work and are still driving on the spare. The woman at the day care snapped at you for being late. Evenings are a blur of fixing dinner, checking school stuff, giving baths, having story time, going through the mail, paying bills, and finally slumping into bed while the news monotones a litany of shootings and car wrecks.

Saturday is catch-up day for housework, laundry, errands, balancing the checkbook, and so on. Your big challenge each month is making ends meet and having no emergencies. Suddenly the doorbell rings. Within minutes a stranger is telling you why the King James Bible is the only version you should read and that the world is going to hell and judgment is around the corner, but if you pray "the prayer" you will be raptured and go up in the sky to meet Jesus—who, by the way, is fairly ticked off with everyone—and would you like to visit his church?

The last time you went to church was years ago, and you couldn't understand what it had to do with anything in life. Boring. Irrelevant. And folks with serious issues and plastered-on smiles. You felt worse after going. Who needs that? The eleven o'clock news makes you feel just as bad, and it lasts only thirty minutes.

And why is this person telling you what you should believe? You don't even know this guy. He could be an ax murderer. And didn't the folks at Waco believe that stuff?

Welcome to the mixed-up world of evangelism. I'm fairly sure that scenario is not what Jesus intended. Instead, what if someone showed up and said, "Hey, we're from such-and-such church, and we're washing cars for free just to show God's love in a practical way. Show me where your spigot is, and we'll hook our hose up and wash your car in your driveway—no strings attached."

Do you think you as that single mom may have a second thought about God—and about his people?

The outward-focused life is rooted in serving, which I believe is a lost language in our current culture of what one futurist once called *cocooning*, a type of social isolationism.

Dr. Christine Pohl, professor of Christian social ethics at Asbury Theological Seminary, said in an interview, "Hospitality in Greek is 'love of strangers.' . . . Welcoming strangers had great significance for the early church. Hospitality meant welcoming outsiders into personal space, mostly a home, and offering them food, shelter, and protection. . . . It had a strong component of recognition and respect—which was most characteristically expressed through shared meals. They understood that who you eat with says a lot about who you . . . value."[1]

I wonder what would happen if once a month you asked someone from your work or school or neighborhood to have dinner with your family or friends. Some of you are dripping with the gift of hospitality but have never recognized that as a power tool from God. Be creative with your gift! I love the Message's version of Romans 12:13: "Be inventive in hospitality."

Another easy way of serving is to practice courtesy. Just simple courtesy. This is a missing social function in our current culture. I consider myself a "people watcher," and because I eat out a lot with others, it fascinates me how little eye contact people make with their server, the one taking the order. It's subliminally Victorian— don't acknowledge the servants.

A smile. A hello. A preferring of someone else at the checkout line. A display of patience at the gas station. This is tough stuff in a consumer-driven, fast-food culture. But it goes a long way. The next time you're in a restaurant, think of this: *HWJO—How Would Jesus Order?* You're not just being a nice guy; you're expressing the servant heart of Jesus in a culture dying for kindness, the language of grace.

Paul wrote to his friend Titus, "No insults, no fights. God's people should be bighearted and courteous" (Titus 3:2 Message). Remember, we're always servants, not just when we're on the clock.

In developing an outward-focused approach to life, sometimes we have to take a look at our irrational inward-focused thoughts. People who are struggling with issues sometimes say things like, "You know, I'm not sure, but I don't feel worthy to talk to God. Why would he listen to me?" I usually respond with, "That's silly. Of course you're not worthy. No one is." That's the power of the personality of God. He chooses to love us in spite of our tediousness, our selfishness, our pettiness, and our sinfulness. But his decision to love us is what makes us infinitely valuable. Apart from God, we're not worthy, but because of his love for us, we're priceless.

That's why it's so important to express our love for our kids. As their "creator," we can give them a sense of worth.

One night when my youngest daughter, Katie, was little, I was sitting on her bed, trying to get her to go to sleep. While we were talking about what we would pray for, we got on the topic of needs and wants. She said, "Dad, I don't get this thing about needs and wants. How do you know the difference?"

"Well," I said, putting on my best pastor voice, "God promises to give us our needs. Those are the things we must have to live, like food and a place to live. Our wants are something different. And sometimes those things aren't really that good for us."

There was a long pause, then she looked at me with those little sleepy eyes and said, "Dad, I need a dog."

So we got a dog.

Later I thought about what Jesus said in Matthew 7: as screwed up as we are, we know how to give gifts to our kids, so how much more will the Father take care of us? It's amazing how free it makes us to love, serve, and give our lives to others when we realize how much we're loved by the only one who gives us true value.

everal years ago, Karla Faye Tucker became the first woman to be executed in Texas in almost 140 years. Hers was a heinous crime—a grisly ax murder. She came from an unbelievably rough drug and prostitution background. While in prison, she had an authentic encounter with Jesus Christ, and her life radically changed. She came to peace with herself and God.

Why should she have been a recipient of God's generosity rather than someone who struggles day in and day out to be a good person? Was that fair to the relatives of the victims? Was it fair that she received God's love? Shouldn't she have suffered?

Former atheist C. S. Lewis once said that it used to puzzle him how Christian writers seemed to be strict at one moment and easy at the next. He wrote, "They talk about mere sins of thought as if they were immensely important: and then they talk about the most frightful murders and treacheries as if you [only had] to repent and all would be forgiven. But I have come to see that they are right."[2]

It's the core of our hearts that Jesus goes to work on. It is the center of us that affects our actions, our behaviors. Sometimes that's where we pastors get it mixed up; we try to change behaviors instead of motivations. A man who is surrendering to Jesus and allowing the Spirit to begin the process of making him more holy will be more and more aware of the badness still inside him. And conversely, a man moving farther away from God, becoming worse internally, understands the evil inside of him less and less. For many of us, after we came to Jesus, little things began to bother us that never did before—a smart-aleck comment that required forgiveness, a thought about someone that needed confession, a little indiscretion in our finances that bugged us. True Christianity is not always a "feel-good" religion. Jesus takes up residence in our hearts and begins to move the furniture around.

Serving others—especially those who don't deserve it—truly reflects the heart of God. I think it makes him smile.

Ernest Gordon was a Christian, author, and former dean of Princeton Seminary who died a few years ago. Gordon was the inspiration behind the movies *Bridge on the River Kwai* and, more recently, *To End All Wars*. He survived three years in one of the most wicked prisoner-of-war camps in Southeast Asia during World War II, where an estimated eighty thousand prisoners died of starvation, dysentery, malaria, and torture while building a railroad. Several hundred men per mile of track died.

Gordon recalled a time at the end of a workday when a shovel was missing from the prison camp toolshed. The brutal officer in charge was furious and announced that the guards would begin shooting each prisoner, one at a time, until the man who took it came forward. As guns were pointed at the first man in line, one of the prisoners stepped out and said, "I did it. I took it." The guards brutally beat him to death in front of everyone. The next day they discovered that they had miscounted—all the shovels were there.

One prisoner remembered the Bible verse, "Greater love hath no man than this, that a man lay down his life for his friends" (John 15:13 KJV). That word spread like wildfire throughout the camp, and the atmosphere changed. Men began treating each other like brothers instead of the grasping, clawing, self-centered animals they had degenerated into. Gordon initiated a Bible study. They started what they called the "church without walls."

Gordon wrote, "Death was still with us—no doubt about that. But we were slowly being freed from its destructive grip. We were seeing for ourselves the sharp contrast between the forces that made for life and those that made for death. Selfishness, hatred, envy, jealousy, greed, self-indulgence, laziness and pride were all anti-life. Love, heroism, self-sacrifice, sympathy, mercy, integrity and creative faith, on the other hand, were the essence of life, turning mere existence into living in its truest sense. These were the gifts of God to men."[3]

Isn't it amazing how a radical act of servanthood can change the atmosphere?

Ashley Smith was all over the news not long ago. Brian Nichols, who had killed four people as he escaped his trial for rape, had forced Smith into her apartment and tied her up. During her seven-and-a-half-hour ordeal, she talked to him about her faith in Jesus, how her husband had died in her arms four years earlier after being stabbed, how she needed to stay alive so her daughter would at least have a mother. But the most impacting moment was when she read a passage from Rick Warren's book *The Purpose Driven Life*. A news article from www.purposedriven.com says:

> Smith asked if she could read to him and reached for her copy of *The Purpose Driven Life*. Her reading for the day said: "We serve God by serving others. . . . In our self-serving culture with its me-first mentality, acting like a servant is not a popular concept. Jesus, however, measured greatness in terms of service, not status. . . . To be like Jesus is to be a servant. That's what he called himself."
>
> It also contains these words, which must have seemed prophetic at the time: "Servants see interruptions as divine appointments for ministry and are happy for the opportunity to practice serving." Being taken hostage at gunpoint by an accused rapist and killer would be an interruption in anybody's book. And serve is what Smith did.
>
> She made breakfast for him: eggs, pancakes, and fruit juice. Finally, Nichols agreed to let her go meet her daughter and asked her to visit him in jail. . . .
>
> He said, "I want to talk to you again."
>
> "You're here in my apartment for some reason," she told him. . . .
>
> He eventually let her go and turned himself in.[4]

Smith later told reporters that God had a purpose in her being taken hostage: "I believe God brought him to my door so he couldn't hurt anyone else."[5]

I don't know if I'd have the courage to do what Ashley Smith did. But it sure made me think about the correlation between interruptions and servanthood.

I magine this New Testament scene: the local ministerial association invites the new itinerant preacher-prophet to a dinner party. Sneaking in the back door and through the kitchen and slipping up behind Jesus is a streetwalker who was well known in town. Not only were women considered second-class and somewhat expendable in society at that time, but this was a prostitute. It didn't get any lower than that culturally. This is not *Pretty Woman*. This is real life: countless men in a filthy bed, STDs with no antibiotics in sight, and a woman's last-ditch attempt to beat poverty by giving her body to any men who had money—men who had not the slightest interest in her emotional bank account, who had become nothing more than talking animals. Can you imagine the risk this woman took to walk into that room of pastors and priests and the well-to-do of religious society—men who lived by a holy, moral code—where prostitutes were stoned to death?

It makes me think about my own life. Am I really ready to risk my reputation in order to love Jesus, to serve him in some way? How about you? Are you willing to risk rejection by your friends, your co-workers? To risk intellectual ridicule? Loving God will always involve a risk.

I think Jesus gives the key to how that kind of passion is unlocked. He turns to the group and says, "He who has been forgiven little loves little" (Luke 7:47). What an odd thing to say in a room full of good, religious, and seemingly together people. Think about how subversive and simple that statement is. He was probing their shallow understanding of the big issue, the great sin of pride—that is, "I have no need of God's forgiveness."

The only way to really love God is to understand the scope of his personal forgiveness offered to us. It's not that we do bad things from time to time; it's that we are so bent on doing whatever we want to do—and that puts us at odds with God's redemptive plan of love for the creatures he loves.

Astronomers are still trying to wrap their cerebrums around the concept of a black hole. A black hole is formed when a massive star burns out all its nuclear fuel, gravity takes over, and the star essentially collapses in on itself. Kind of like Elvis. It is thought that a massive star, ten to twenty times larger than our sun, can actually compress into something smaller than a pinpoint, with a gravitational pull so strong that not even light can escape—an invisible, light-bending powerhouse of compressed gravity, a cosmic Hoover vacuum that sucks in space itself.

Let me give you an emotional and spiritual black hole: we're worth something when we're performing well and others approve of us. This is a black hole on two counts: our value is based on our performance and others' opinions of us. That will bend the truth and suck in the light.

Here's a biblical view: we're worth something when we know what God really thinks of us and how he values us. What we think about God is not nearly as important as finding out what he thinks about us. And once we find that out, it makes sense that we should make ourselves accountable to him for applying that truth to our lives on a regular basis.

In other words, we are valuable because God values us. As a matter of fact, we are of so much value to God—even when we were neck-deep in self-serving, inward-focused sin—that he gave his Son for us. The Phillips translation of Romans 5:8 says, "The proof of God's amazing love is this: that it was while we were sinners that Christ died for us." Did you catch that? God placed an inestimable value on us before we were even regenerated. The truth is that God loves us apart from what we've done, who we are, and what we will ever do. Once we get that, we're on our way to understanding grace. And grace is the one distinction Christianity has from every other world religion.

Our value isn't based on what we do or what others think of us but only on God's love for us. And that's why we are so free to be the lowest rung on the social ladder: servants.

You know the old story of Jonah and the fish. I believe Jonah is a microcosmic picture of the church. The church is just a collection of ex-beggars who've tasted God's mercy and have enough left over in brown bags for anyone else who's hungry.

Jonah was given a message for the hated enemies of Israel, the Assyrians. The Assyrians were a fast-growing world power. They were well known for being merciless. Archaeologists have uncovered writings in which they brag about their cruelty—skinning alive prisoners of war, burning children to death, stacking pyramids of human skulls just to psych out their enemies. And they hated the Jews.

With that context, Jonah, a Jewish prophet, was told to go and warn the Assyrian city of Nineveh that if they didn't stop their violence, God was going to take them down. Now what would you do if you were Jonah and these were the people who were prophesied to pillage your family, land, and country?

You'd probably do what Jonah did: go the opposite direction. But after a little midcourse correction involving a big fish, Jonah went to Nineveh.

He gave the message, the people actually repented, and God had mercy on them. Jonah knew that his hated enemies were spared, and he "was furious. He lost his temper. He yelled at God, 'God! I knew it—when I was back home, I knew this was going to happen! That's why I ran off to Tarshish! I knew you were sheer grace and mercy, not easily angered, rich in love, and ready at the drop of a hat to turn your plans of punishment into a program of forgiveness!'" (Jonah 4:1–2 Message).

God is merciful—even to our morally wrong, corrupt enemies. We don't have a clue how rich his mercy is. We don't get it. And like Jonah, if we're honest we'd rather see the people who deserve to get wiped out get wiped out.

Get personal for a moment. Who has done you wrong, done your family wrong, done your career wrong? If you knew God was giving him or her an opportunity to receive his mercy and love, would you deliver the message?

Here's another question for you: who is your enemy and how have you responded?

Like a servant?

One Saturday night we had a crack in the main water line of our church building. Water was gushing into the building. It was a long night trying to figure out what we could do before the Sunday morning celebrations. At 1:30 a.m. Sunday morning, I finally headed home, thinking about how this was going to work, feeling pretty tired, and remembering I had to get up in five hours and do three more celebrations. I was flying down the road when all of a sudden, blue lights came on behind me. A policeman pulled me over and said, "Do you know what you were doing?"

"Yes, sir," I said. "I was driving really, really fast."

He asked, "Where are you going?"

"I'm almost home. I can almost see it from here."

Then he said, "What's going on?"

I replied, "Do you really want to know?" He nodded. I started whining, "I pastor at the Vineyard and we had a water main break and I've been there all day today and muddy water was pouring in and a lot of people are coming in a few hours and blah blah blah . . ." He just wrote the ticket. I thought, *Where's the love? Where's the mercy?*

Now it would have been classic if I had gone to court and the judge, when hearing this case, had said, "The city law enforcement is absolutely right. This guy was dangerous and could have hurt himself or someone else. He broke the law and deserves to pay this enormous fine of $130. But I love this guy, and I want to show him God's love in a practical way. In order for justice to take place and the righteous demands of the law to be met, I'm going to take off my royal robe, step into his shoes, and pay his fine with my own money."

Justice and mercy meet. And that's exactly what God did on our behalf. He paid the fine; we walk. When we understand that, it should make us want to do something for someone else who also perhaps doesn't deserve it.

Unforgiveness is a prison with the lock on our side and the key in our hand. Most of us have something in our lives that we would give anything to go back and change. We would never have married that jerk who walked out on us. Or never told that so-called friend a vulnerable secret they blabbed to everybody. Or trusted a co-worker with something they took credit for. Or been the victim of a stranger's road rage, or racism, or random violence, or abuse.

In the arena of forgiveness, though, Christians have a unique vantage point. They understand that there's a deep well of personal forgiveness from which they've drunk. There is nothing more powerful than the real-life, in-your-face expression of forgiveness than Jesus, who, after being stripped and beaten, having a crown of thorns jammed into his skin, being forced to carry his own cross up a bare hill, being stretched out upon that cross with spikes through his bruised flesh, and being hoisted up to die an excruciating death, still said, "Father, forgive them; they don't know what they're doing" (Luke 23:34 Message). It's the ultimate expression of love.

Let me tell you what I'd do if someone did that to one of my kids and I was God: this place would be called "the planet formerly known as Earth." I'd light myself a big old cosmic cigar off the glowing ember that was once this world if you touched my kid. But I'm not God. Neither are you. And life is way better because of that, even though some of us will be surprised when scientists discover the center of the universe and find we're not there.

If all of us are in need of forgiveness—and the foundation of Christianity is that we've all screwed up—then you can guarantee that all of us have a need to forgive someone else. And if we don't, we imprison ourselves. In a creepy way, we lock ourselves inside with the person who caused the pain, their ghost rattling the chains of pain from time to time. Forgiveness may be the ultimate act of serving, but it is the most freeing for ourselves.

I hope I don't sound like a naysayer, but it's my belief that the average church in America cannot exist much longer in its current form—in practice, not in theology. In his classic book *What's So Amazing About Grace?* Philip Yancey writes:

> Recently I have been asking a question of strangers: "When I say the words 'evangelical Christian' what comes to mind?" In reply, mostly I hear political descriptions: of strident pro-life activists, or gay-rights opponents, or proposals for censoring the internet. I hear references to the Moral Majority, an organization disbanded years ago. Not once—not once—have I heard a description . . . of grace. Apparently that is not the aroma Christians give off in the world.[6]

It's not that those things Yancey mentioned are bad. But it's sad when the one thing that makes Christianity unique among the world religions—that is, grace, the undeserved favor of God—is not even mildly apparent. If we are known only for being the moral police, then something is wrong. Yancey quotes Jewish intellectual Anthony Hecht:

> Over the years I . . . became increasingly acquainted with the convictions of my Christian neighbors. Many of these were good people whom I admire, and from whom I learned goodness itself, among other things. And there was much in Christian doctrine that seemed appealing as well. But few things struck me with more force than the profound and unappeasable hostility of Protestants and Catholics toward one another.[7]

What's wrong with this picture? I'm not looking for some vague ecumenicism. I'm looking for some evidence of the grace of God among believers. Could it be that our churches are dying because no one can get in the door to receive God's love unless they look like us, behave like us, and talk like us? Are we identified by our love for the lost—whom Jesus gave his life for—or by our denominations? Could it be we are lumbering dinosaurs in a culture dying for God's love, protecting our crusty armor while waddling into extinction? I think God has destined us for something far greater.

Grace can be expressed in the simplest ways by serving someone who probably doesn't deserve it. And I think that's most of us.

My friend Mark Lutz oversees all of our growth and healing groups at the church, focusing on recovery and support. He grew up in a very different environment than me—a Christian home. He told me that as he grew up in church, people would say, "You have to guard your Christian witness." This meant you had to make sure no one saw you doing anything that would reflect poorly on Jesus.

He gave it his best shot, but what he discovered was this: he wasn't too good at being good. His attempt to guard his Christian witness put him in a bind: to pretend to be better than he was or admit that he was a failure as a Christian.

He increased his attempts to be better while pretending to be good enough, but that felt hypocritical. The fruit of this obsession with his goodness, or lack of it, was that he became very inward focused.

Mark told me, "Everything was about me, my latest sin, my latest improvement, the short-lived nature of my latest improvement. The only outward thoughts I had were to compare myself with someone else. I was relieved when I read in 1 Timothy 1, 'Here is a trustworthy saying that deserves full acceptance: Christ Jesus came into the world to save sinners—of whom I am the worst. But for that very reason I was shown mercy so that in me, the worst of sinners, Christ Jesus might display his unlimited patience as an example for those who would believe on him and receive eternal life'" (vv. 15–16).

Mark continued, "I learned this: people outside of the church weren't attracted to God when they thought I was so good. When I admitted that I had the same Christian witness as the apostle Paul—that I'm just a sinner caught by the mercy of Christ—people connected with that and wanted to know more. And I discovered that when I wasn't self-absorbed in my own attempts at goodness, I had the emotional and mental energy to listen to them, care about them, and introduce them to my friend Jesus."

Mark's a pretty wise guy, wouldn't you say?

The great enemy of grace is religion. I mean religion in its most negative state. Jesus had his biggest conflicts with religious people—and religious leaders at that. Of course, none of us ever thinks we're *that* kind of religious person.

The problem with religion is that it deceptively moves our hearts away from grace, and it becomes all about performance. Years ago I was leading worship as a volunteer, and as I would drive to church each Sunday to lead, I would go into hyperfaith. That is, if I didn't pray in the Spirit for thirty minutes before leading worship, then worship wasn't going to happen. And if it didn't happen, it was my fault.

One Sunday morning as I was in hyperfaith—praying in the Spirit at about ninety miles an hour—God broke in and said, "You really think this thing depends on you, don't you?" In other words, if I didn't pray just right, then God wouldn't show up. I suddenly realized how sick I was, how religious, how egocentric, how much I left out the body of Christ and the beauty of grace.

And so for the next month or so, I'd drive to church with a heavy metal station playing at 120 decibels—just to drive out the religious demons. And it worked.

I heard a story about a church in a small town where one woman was the self-appointed morality police, using gossip as her weapon. One day she accused Bob, a new believer in the church, of being an alcoholic after she saw his pickup truck parked in front of the town's bar one afternoon. Well, it got back to Bob. So that evening he parked his pickup truck in front of the woman's house, walked home, and left it there all night.

Let's be careful not to mix performance with grace. It's easy to develop a religion that limits God's love to how well we perform. That doesn't mean we should become morally or spiritually sloppy, but we shouldn't tie what we do to God's capacity to love us. Remember, if we express grace only to those who deserve it, it's no longer grace but wages. And that's something very different.

Collection Six

The Ultimate Servant

Often people in our church go out in teams and do free things for people just to serve them—anything from a car wash to a bottle of water to cleaning restrooms for area businesses.

Some years back I was with a team of pastors in England, and we were teaching them how to clean the loo—the restroom—in pubs and businesses. This was during a conference, and there were lots of different denominations there. We walked into one office, and a proper British woman greeted us at the door. Like the proper American I am, I blurted out, "Hey, we're here to clean your loo for free today."

She said, "Who are you people?" I told her we were Christians from all sorts of churches and rattled off some of the church names. She asked why we wanted to clean the restroom for free, so I gave our standard answer: "Just to show you God's love in a simple way—no strings attached." I handed her a little card that said basically the same thing, and she said, "I'll have to ask my supervisor." She disappeared into a board room where I could just barely see some suits sitting around a table. As they passed the card around to each person, I could hear them laughing and asking, "They want to what?" *This is way too much fun*, I thought.

The woman eventually came back out and said, "No thanks. We have professional cleaners come each day."

"No problem. You have a nice day." I turned to walk away.

She looked at the card again and said, "Tell me again: why do you clean toilets?"

"We just want to serve people to express God's love for us."

She seemed so puzzled. She looked at me and said, "Well, I'm a Methodist, and we don't clean toilets."

I replied, "Uh . . . this isn't a doctrinal statement."

She paused, and then I could almost see a lightbulb go on above her head. She smiled and said, "You know, I guess if Jesus were here today, maybe instead of washing feet he would clean a restroom."

Brilliant, as the Brits say.

For whom did Jesus die?

When I slow down long enough to see the pettiness and self-consumed dynamic of my life and the beauty of my Father's love for me, I'm honestly surprised that he would choose to love me. I love it when Jesus tells his friends, "You did not choose me, but I chose you" (John 15:16). Or sometimes I think about how magnanimous it is that God lets us enter into relationship with him after we say things like, "Well, I've tried everything else. I might as well try Jesus." I'm amazed that he'll take us into his arms even after that self-centered dismissal.

For whom did Jesus die?

A young guy with seriously gauged ears came up to me after one of our celebrations and said, "I feel like I'm supposed to show God's love to the Gay & Lesbian Community Center here, but I'm not sure what to do, and I'm honestly a little self-conscious about going there myself. What would my friends say if they saw me? What would they think?"

I said, "Let's go clean the bathrooms there. They've probably never had a church do that." He gave me the biggest smile and said, "I'm in!"

Gays and lesbians are simply people for whom Jesus died. My toilet-cleaning friend was thrilled to clean the restrooms, and they seemed to be too when we showed up on Saturday to clean the restrooms at their community center. Did anyone "come to Christ" in a classical way that day? I don't think so, but they received me. And I don't fully know how this works, but Jesus did say, "He who receives you receives me" (Matt. 10:40). It may be just one more nudge toward the Father.

In 1 Corinthians 6, Paul writes:

> Surely you know that the people who do wrong will not inherit God's kingdom. Do not be fooled. Those who sin sexually, worship idols, take part in adultery, those who are male prostitutes, or men who have sexual relations with other men, those who steal, are

greedy, get drunk, lie about others, or rob—these people will not inherit God's kingdom. In the past, some of you were like that, but you were washed clean.

vv. 9–11 NCV

What a great reminder: "Some of you were like that."
For whom did Jesus die?

Sometimes people mistake the outward-focused life and serving others with being nice. Nothing could be further from the truth. Don't misunderstand me; kindness is a potent weapon. It was Paul who wrote to the Romans that it is God's kindness that leads us toward repentance. But that's not necessarily the same as being nice.

Jesus didn't come to make us nice people. He parachuted into enemy-occupied territory to liberate us. His was a D-day mission. He came to do battle. The Bible is clear in 1 John 3:8: "The Son of God appeared for this purpose, to destroy the works of the devil" (NASB).

Until we understand that Jesus confronted a malevolent spiritual force—and that we are in the same conflict—we really don't understand Christianity. That's why having a "nice" church doesn't cut it for me. If I'm not seeing people being set free, being transformed, I'm out of there. And birthing spiritual babies is messy, just like natural birth is. That place of repentance is often where spiritual conflict takes place, both in prayer and in servanthood. Serving others is one of the most powerful spiritual weapons we have. And you know why? Because it's not natural to the culture, and it's supernatural in origin. As Paul wrote, "The weapons of our warfare are not natural, but powerful for pulling down strongholds" (2 Cor. 10:4 author's paraphrase).

There is probably nothing more unnatural than serving lost people with no strings attached in this me-first culture. Service is a prevailing weapon for the church that expresses grace—that ultimate spoiler of satanic strategies—in a simple but dramatic way. Try it yourself; you may experience a fair amount of spiritual warfare the first time you initiate some simple service outreaches in your church.

And don't say I didn't tell you it may get messy.

Several years ago during a day of prayer and fasting in our church for our city, Sharon Karns, one of our pastors on the senior leadership team at that time, said she got a picture, a vision of sorts, that was compelling. She remembered the news stories after 9/11 of the people in New York City roaming around the perimeter of the rubble of the twin towers with pictures of missing loved ones. They would talk to reporters, rescue workers, and anyone who was around the site, holding up pictures of missing friends and family members. They would describe things about them, brag about them, and talk about the things they loved about them. And weep over them. You'd see them on the news each day, asking and searching for any news about their loved one.

In Sharon's vision, she saw something similar, but with Jesus instead of those people. He was holding up his hands, and all over his fingers and palms were little pictures of missing people. He would describe them, the details of their lives, and all the things he loved about them.

You and I get to take part in finding missing people—people the Father is looking for. Think of that—you and me, of all people. We get to help him. I remember once losing my youngest daughter in a jam-packed mall during the Christmas season. After we called security, I ran through the mall, darting into stores and screaming for my little girl. As I headed down one wing, I looked up and saw a smiling woman with her hands on Katie's shoulders, standing in place, knowing that a frantic father was coming her way. I can't tell you how grateful I was for that woman who had stood by my little girl, keeping her calm, while her friend had gone to get a security guard. What a servant.

I wonder if that's how our heavenly Father feels when one of us finds a missing child and brings them to him. How thrilled he must be to have someone looking for lost children. Having an outward focus keeps us centered on the fact that our primary job in the church is doing just that. And serving opens the door to make finding them possible.

No one has lived life more decisively than Jesus. Think about it: even prior to his becoming a man, we are told in Philippians 2 that his entering the human race was a decisive act of servant love, that he consciously emptied himself to be born into the womb of a backwoods young woman and face the world from a feeding trough for barn animals.

In Luke 2 we find the only childhood reference to Jesus in Scripture. His whole family, along with relatives, comes to Jerusalem for the Passover. Afterward they load up all the minivans and head for home, but by the time they reach the Motel 6 they discover that twelve-year-old Jesus is missing. He's not with Uncle Zechariah. Aunt Elizabeth hasn't seen him. And then his parents panic.

Have you ever lost a kid in the mall? Then you know the feeling. But what if you lost God's Son? That's pretty serious! How do you explain that to some angel who shows up at your door? "We all got sheep burgers at McFalafel's, then we turned around and, hey, he was gone!" Mary and Joseph spent three days looking for Jesus and finally found him in the synagogue in Jerusalem, talking with the rabbis. They were furious! But again, would you spank God's Son? They use the typical "guilting" parent line: "Why have you treated us like this?" (Luke 2:48). And what was his reply? "Why were you searching for me? . . . Didn't you know I had to be in my Father's house?" (v. 49). Already at age twelve Jesus was finding his focus, his reason to exist.

Years later, "some Pharisees came to Jesus and said to him, 'Leave this place and go somewhere else. Herod wants to kill you.' He replied, 'Go tell that fox, "I will drive out demons and heal people today and tomorrow, and on the third day I will reach my goal." In any case, I must keep going today and tomorrow and the next day—for surely no prophet can die outside Jerusalem!'" (Luke 13:31–33).

Jesus knew he was born to die. His support group said, "Go anywhere but Jerusalem." But rather than reacting to their fear, he set his sights on his goal.

And, of course, it was an outward-focused goal: you and me.

The Community of Servants

Sometimes I see an us-against-them mentality creep into the church. In that mode, all of the world is in two camps, and we can never have any interaction with people outside of our camp. "They" are all wrong. And so the church takes on a siege mentality and becomes a fortress rather than a force in the world.

Perhaps a healthier approach to expressing God's heart to those "outside" is by serving them. It's not us against them; it's us serving them. Jesus told a story in which people turned down invitations to come to a man's party. So the man told his employees, "Go to the country roads. Whoever you find, drag them in. I want my house full!" (Luke 14:23 Message). Sometimes we forget that God is the one throwing the party and it's his guest list, not ours.

One time after teaching in a particular area of Judea, Jesus left for open country. But the crowds went looking and, when they found him, clung to him so he couldn't go on. He told them, "Don't you realize that there are yet other villages where I have to tell the Message of God's kingdom, that this is the work God sent me to do?" (Luke 4:42 Message).

We want to circle the wagons and say "us four and no more." We're against those wicked Democrats or blood-sucking Republicans. Or those mixed-up people in that other religion. Or those folks who are anti-life. Or those pro–free speech/pornography people. Or those people who look different than us.

Sometimes we forget they're all people Jesus died for; they're invaluable to him. And somehow Jesus was able to slip into that world and move about without being tainted. Even to the point that he was mocked as being a friend of sinners. I long that our churches—the very body of Christ upon the earth—become known as the friends of sinners.

Someday I'd love to see this on some big church sign: First ABC Community Church, Friend of Sinners. How good would that be?

One September day I was sitting in my favorite Mexican restaurant with Anita and said, "I just can't do another Christmas Eve program again. I'm sick of them. . . . I'm going to cancel it this year."

She choked on her fajita and said, "You can't do that!" She looked at me like I had said, "Let's put the X back in Xmas."

I reminded her, "I'm the pastor. Are you sure?" I was just tired of a big show. And then Anita reminded me of something that had changed my life. Back in 1984 we did our first outreach as a brand-new little church of twenty-five people. We gave away a few bags of groceries and Christmas trees in the projects. We were so naïve that we would knock on the doors and ask if there were any poor people there. There were several dynamics that happened: not only was there a need being met, but there was a shift in the way people—mostly estranged from church—saw Christians. Better yet, they saw the kingdom of God crashing into their world. We were hooked.

Suddenly my wife said, "Why don't we do an outreach on Christmas Eve?"

I mulled over that for a few minutes and then said, "Hey, I've got a great idea: why don't we do an outreach on Christmas Eve?" She just smiled and took another bite of her fajita.

It has now become a tradition for us. Instead of a big production, we buy thousands of boxes of Krispy Kreme doughnuts and pass them out to all who come Christmas Eve night, with this mandate: go out and give them to people who have to work on Christmas Eve—those at police stations, fire stations, video stores, hospitals, and so on.

Afterward, one woman told me this story: "We went to Taco Bell and actually cut in front of the car who was ordering. After giving the cashier our doughnuts, we told her we also wanted to pay the bill for the car behind us. She wanted to know why. When we told her and gave her a card to give to them, she was so happy that she grabbed my hand and said, 'God bless you, God bless you!' She was so pleased and said she loved me. Then the people in the car waved to us. It was so awesome to bring that joy to so many in one night, especially at the saddest and loneliest time of year for so many."

We have a mantra in our church: it's not about us, it's about Jesus . . . and others.

What I like about developing an outward-focused view of life is that it allows for "baby steps" toward learning to serve people who don't yet know Jesus. I remember a friend of mine who talked to his church about wanting to do a simple outreach. He had been funding outreaches for his friends and family to do but thought his church might want to get involved in the next one. He was told it would be brought before the evangelism committee. After weeks passed, he was told they would probably approve of it and be ready to launch it—in three years. "Three years?" he said. "I was thinking about next month!" Planning is good. But sometimes we can use that as an excuse to never really do anything.

Rick Warren writes, "Most churches are over-managed and under-led. Your church needs to be managed, but it also needs to be led. You have to have both. When you only have management in the church, you get the problem of paralysis of analysis. It's like 'Ready . . . Aim . . . Aim . . . Aim. . . .' And they never fire. Management without leadership results in constantly analyzing and looking. . . . You need managers within the church as well. Without them you end up with a church that says, 'Ready . . . Fire!' without ever taking the time to aim. You need both."[1]

I tend to think that most of our churches are in the first mode. Sometimes I think we're so paralyzed by thinking we have to be super prepared, super trained, and super apologetically superior that we forget that love is the key—and real love knows that somehow, in the economy of God, it never fails. To do a Coke giveaway on a busy street corner, all the training you need is learning how to say "Regular or Diet?" and to stay out of the street.

Mary Lyon was a passionate Christian who practically single-handedly raised funds to launch the first seminary for women to be trained for ministry in 1837. She encouraged others to trust in God—and do something. I like that. It's easier to turn the steering wheel of a car when it's moving than when it's sitting still.

I say we get started doing something when it comes to serving people who don't yet know Jesus. There are lots of simple projects to get started that cost very little.

Maybe it's not resources that stop us, but a simple fear of that first baby step.

I believe the Bible teaches that we become more whole, more fulfilled, as our focus moves away from ourselves and more toward the Father. That's why Jesus told his disciples not to worry about what they would wear or what they would eat, that if they would focus on what the Father was doing instead, all of those things would be taken care of. That's a really radical outward focus. I've met very few people who actually function like that—and I thought some of them needed medication.

But all Jesus was doing was juxtaposing an inward-focused approach to life with an outward focus on God and others. Physician John Andrew Holmes wrote, "It is well to remember that the entire population of the universe, with one trifling exception, is composed of others."[2]

The Bible describes life that is lived inwardly in a depressing way:

> It is obvious what kind of life develops out of trying to get your own way all the time: repetitive, loveless, cheap sex; a stinking accumulation of mental and emotional garbage; frenzied and joyless grabs for happiness; trinket gods; magic-show religion; paranoid loneliness; cutthroat competition; all-consuming-yet-never-satisfied wants; a brutal temper; an impotence to love or be loved; divided homes and divided lives; small-minded and lopsided pursuits; the vicious habit of depersonalizing everyone into a rival; uncontrolled and uncontrollable addictions; ugly parodies of community. I could go on.
>
> This isn't the first time I have warned you, you know. If you use your freedom this way, you will not inherit God's kingdom.
>
> Galatians 5:19–21 Message

Developing an outward-focused approach to life will slowly begin to change everything, even the way a church looks and functions. When we really believe that life is not about us but all about Jesus and other people, when we intentionally develop an atmosphere of grace and acceptance, and when we say "come as you are" in our churches, it's going to get messy. Really messy.

I always find it interesting when someone gets mad about something at the Vineyard and tells me we should be more like the New Testament church, as if that was some idyllic time in church history. My response is, "Which New Testament church do you want to be like? The Corinthians were having sex every which way you can, suing each other, and getting drunk at church potlucks. People in the Thessalonian church were quitting their jobs and sitting around waiting for Jesus to return. Folks in the Colossian church were worshiping angels and beating themselves to prove how holy they were. In the Galatian church people were turning into legalists and racists. So which New Testament church do you want to be like?"

Every church has issues to deal with. As a pastor, I often see people who have come from other churches, and sometimes I hear things like, "Wow! This is such a great church. This is everything I'm looking for!" I usually stop them right there and ask if they would like me to alphabetize all the stuff that's screwed up here and drives me crazy. There's no perfect church because there are no perfect Christians. That's why we need a perfect Savior.

But one thing is clear: if you make it a goal to develop an outward-focused church to serve those who don't yet know Jesus, it's eventually going to be messy, because people are—especially people in process. But I'd much rather have that than neat and tidy.

For me, the goal is unity, not conformity.

One of my all-time favorite proverbs is Proverbs 14:4: "Where no oxen are, the manger is clean, but much revenue comes by the strength of the ox" (NASB). In other words, if you want a clean barn, don't have cows. But you won't have any income either.

In my world, that translates as: if you want a clean church, don't birth any new Christians. As a matter of fact, have as few people as possible because they'll leave a mess. People are messy. But if you want new life, it won't be tidy.

When our kids were younger, our little mop dog, Lucy, had pups. Lucy is from a breed of dogs I can't say because it sounds like I'm cussing. Anita thought that our kids seeing Lucy give birth would be a great experience for them. I'm telling you, it was a messy experience. When she started having her first pup, I ran to the school to get our kids out. I told the receptionist that I needed to take them out for the day because our dog was having babies. She just looked at me and said, "Whatever."

Have you ever seen a dog give birth? It's messy. No, it's gross. I'll spare you the gory details, but it did involve eating everything. Usually twice. After the third pup was born and Lucy started to clean up, I said to my wife, "You know, I think I'll just go watch TV for a while. . . . I'd rather watch *Jeopardy* reruns than this."

Anita smiled and replied, "Dave, she knows exactly what to do. This is totally natural."

I said, "You didn't do that."

I'm convinced men are way more wimpy about this stuff than women. If we were the ones who had to have the babies, there would be no population problem. Every night we would say, "Uh, honey, I've got a headache."

New life is messy. New believers are messy. People seeking God are messy. And they make old believers messy. When our own kids were born, they were a messy disruption in our young married life. Show me a nice, emotionally tidy church, and I'll show you a church that isn't growing.

No cows, no mess. But no life either.

I think the church has always struggled with the tension between evangelism and holiness. I have friends who say when it comes to evangelism, anything short of sin is fair. That's not a bad rule of thumb! We need to be wise: if our non-Christian friends are influencing us more than we're influencing them, we need to disentangle ourselves. But if that change comes out of a holier-than-thou mind-set, we're headed for trouble. As Jonathan Edwards wrote, "Spiritual pride disposes persons to stand at a distance from others, as better than they. . . . [Spiritual pride] is the most secret of all sins."

I love how practical the apostle Paul is on this. In 1 Corinthians 5 he says, "When I wrote to you before, I told you not to associate with people who indulge in sexual sin. But I wasn't talking about unbelievers who indulge in sexual sin, or who are greedy or are swindlers or idol worshipers. You would have to leave this world to avoid people like that" (vv. 9–10 NLT).

Did you read between the lines there? What is he saying about what was going on in the church? When he told them not to associate with greedy people or people messing around sexually, he wasn't talking about non-Christians! We need to remember that church is messy because people are messy.

We have a calling to serve those who haven't yet surrendered to Jesus. God has called the church to be a force, not a fortress. This is not about circling the wagons. One of the reasons Jesus was persecuted was because of who he hung out with. "The Pharisees and religion scholars were not pleased, not at all pleased. They growled, 'He takes in sinners and eats meals with them, treating them like old friends'" (Luke 15:2 Message).

The mission at our church is simple: to love the people of our city into relationship with Jesus. That means rubbing shoulders with those who are outside the body.

And when that happens, there's one thing I know for sure: it won't be a tidy church.

True pastor confession time here: I'm a mega-introvert and am goofy enough to think I could easily find bliss alone in a room with my notebook computer, DVDs, Pringles, and Diet Dr. Pepper. I could cocoon like crazy if it wasn't for the kingdom of God and my wife inviting friends over all the time. I'm embarrassed to tell that; I'm pretty sure that pastors are supposed to be a lot more shepherd-like than that.

But even with a shallow gene pool and my own self-developed weirdness, oddly enough, the older I get the more deeply I feel and recognize my need for others.

Organizational consultant and author Peter Senge writes about a greeting that is used among the tribes of KwaZulu-Natal in South Africa. When two people meet, instead of saying "hello," one person says, "I see you." The other person then answers a single word that means "I am here." Senge writes, "The order of the exchange is important. . . . It's as if, when you see me, you bring me into existence."[3] There is a saying among the tribes that "a person is a person because of other people." I like that. That's community.

Sometimes people will say to me, "You know, I don't really like going to church. I feel closer to God if I'm taking a walk in the woods by myself. Me and nature . . . that's how I feel closest to God." I can understand that. But there's one thing wrong with this picture: it's all about you and what you get out of it. The reality is that you have something to offer the body of Christ, and someone isn't receiving it because you're not there to give it. To use the apostle Paul's analogy of the body, you might be a kidney, and we need you. Believe me, the body needs a kidney.

That's why developing an outward-focused approach to your walk with Jesus is critical. And that's why I talk so much about some disciplined routines for serving others.

One of our small group leaders in the suburbs sent us an email following Halloween:

Our Halloween party in our yard was a huge success! My wife and I lead two different small groups for singles that partnered together and built the games, donated over 180 pounds of candy, passed out invitations on Saturday to the 250 houses in our neighborhood, and then came early to set up and work the party.

For a while you could not see the grass or concrete driveway because there were so many kids and parents there. It was amazing! I was able to meet a lot of my neighbors, and they were thankful for us putting on the party. . . . There were somewhere between 400 and 500 kids and family members that visited.

We gave away about 175 bottles of water, 4 gallons of hot chocolate, 100 Pringles individual packs, 90 hot dogs, 90 Cat-in-the-Hat plush toys, 140 Polaroid pictures of the kids in their costumes, and over 170 pounds of candy. Notice that we count the candy not in bags but in pounds.

The kids would come to our driveway and be greeted with a small bag of candy with our church business card in it, then "Cinderella" took their picture. Then they would take 5, 10, even 20 minutes to play a game and get a handful of candy, then win the game and get another handful of candy . . . then play other games.

This whole event in making the games and throwing the party was a great gift to the neighborhood, while it also has been a catalyst in helping build friendships across our groups, using people's talents and growing disciples, as these two singles small groups banded together to make this happen in only three weeks! What a privilege to lead small groups that have such great servants of God!

Wow. . . . I'm worn out, but what a fun and blessed time. God is already working in my neighbors' lives because of this small act of kindness in showing God's love in a practical way!

Did serving foster a sense of community in this small group, or did a sense of community foster serving? Now there's a philosophical conundrum.

For years I've held on to a letter that reminds me of what's really important. A woman wrote to me:

We live on a busy street. There are a lot of kids who ride by our house on their bikes. I am probably overly protective of my children because I don't want them to get in with the wrong crowd. Perhaps not a very Christlike move on my part, but I feel I need to protect them. There is a little girl who rides around here named Annie. I have had to talk to her before, because she turns our water spigot on until she has made a mudhole of our yard. She is always dirty, and I, ashamedly so, hate to see her coming. [My six-year-old daughter] Becky was outside playing today, and her older sister came inside to tell on her. Becky was playing with Annie. I told my older daughter to ask Becky to come inside for a minute. I asked Becky why she was playing with Annie.

She said, "Mom, I am playing with her because she has no friends. She rides by here every day by herself and never has anybody with her. I thought that I would not like to have to ride my bike alone all day, so I asked her if I could be her friend. She is sitting out on our porch right now waiting for me. Can I go back out and play with her?"

I was dumbfounded. I get so wrapped up in what I am doing and in trying to raise good kids that I forget what God wants us to be doing. I took a Popsicle out to Annie, and she thanked me and smiled the prettiest little smile through that dirty face. Then I thought of that verse about "whatever you do to the least of these, you do to me."

This letter makes me think about what's really important in my life. And maybe I should stop asking, "What's important?" and start asking, "Who's important?" "Who" is always more important than "what." The question all of us have to ask is, "How important to us are people who don't yet know Jesus?" There are adults who ride their bikes past the doors of our churches each day and don't know that Jesus—the friend of sinners—is their friend. They have dirty lives and play in dirty mudholes, and we, the church, have all the Popsicles.

We just need to step off the porch and ask them if they'll be our friend.

We recently got a great letter from Steve North, the pastor of a small-town church in central Ohio. He came to one of our Servant Evangelism Weekend Intensives, and his church did their first outreach two weeks later. He wrote:

> We had twelve students and three adults split up into three groups. One group went to the five businesses in our town that are open on Sunday afternoons, including two bars. That group said it was like E. F. Hutton speaking when they offered the [employees] small boxes of candy and a connection card with the words, "This is our way of letting you know that God loves you." I'm pretty sure no church people had ever been to either of those places for that purpose before. They were received with thanks.
>
> The other two groups went to strip shopping centers in Chillicothe, a town about nine miles from ours. Both of these groups experienced retail clerks, who had been inundated with rushed and sometimes discourteous customers, bursting out in tears or other similar responses. This happened more than once. A woman working alone in a shoe store wrote me a two-page letter about how she was moved to tears . . . and the difference it made in her life to be reminded of God's love for her on a difficult day like that one. I received a second letter from another store employee a few days later.
>
> Three sisters in our youth ministry went home that night and told their mother about what we had done. Hearing about it moved her to tears as well. The next day, Valentine's Day, she went to her job at a florist shop and told all the employees about our outreach. [She said] the entire day was changed for the employees in that store, as a sense of God's care for them remained through the day. She shared this story in church the next Sunday morning after the students had talked about their experience. I never did get to preach that day as the place came unglued—people praying for those who had been touched, for our youth and children, and for each other.

Would to God that the whole "Big C" Church would come unglued as we serve lost people. That might beat any sermon we could give.

Many times in praying with people in our church who are going through tough times, I'll ask them what kind of support they have around them. In other words, do they have other believers who know what they're going through and are praying for them and walking with them? The majority of the time they'll say no. Of course I'll pray for them, but there's something missing in that whole equation, and something that hinders what God could do in their lives.

It's interesting what is implied in Jesus's parable of the lost sheep. It was lost not only from the shepherd but also from the flock. The prodigal son was estranged not only from the father but also from the father's household. The people who turned down dinner invitations didn't want to be a part of the master's party. The kingdom of God is referenced by our connection with a group of other people.

When I was ten years old, I was riding my bike down the street, trying to outrace a train at a railroad crossing. I flew across the tracks just in front of the train as the engineer blasted the horn at me. I was feeling pretty cool until I stopped my bike and looked up to see my Aunt Lizabelle standing on her porch, arms crossed, with a serious look. She said quietly, "Don't you ever do that again. You could have slipped and been cut in two! I ought to tell your mother." I turned bright red and felt ashamed. I never did that again. I knew that Aunt Lizabelle loved me. I think it really does take a community to raise a child.

Community is more than warm, fuzzy feelings or harmony. There is a spiritual and emotional safety in it. The church word for that is *accountability*, but that sounds stiff and cold. I have no interest in sitting across a table with someone who asks me, "How have you messed up this week?" Accountability is not the goal; being known is.

Part of becoming outward focused means we take the leap into community. As the apostle Paul wrote in Romans 14: "None of us lives to himself alone and none of us dies to himself alone" (v. 7).

Every once in a while at the Vineyard a person of color will tell me how they were ignored, were left with their hand out instead of shaken, were not acknowledged, or were met with some other degree of rudeness. I'll apologize and usually say that when we invite people to "come as you are," people actually come as they are, with agendas, pain, bigotries, issues, prejudices, and whatever else. That's no great excuse, but it was even that way in the early church.

The book of Acts describes a form of bigotry in the first century: "As the number of disciples grew, Greek-speaking Jews complained about the Hebrew-speaking Jews. The Greek-speaking Jews claimed that the widows among them were neglected every day when food and other assistance was distributed" (Acts 6:1 GOD'S WORD®). In other words, "You Hebrew-speaking Jews are ignoring our Greek-speaking Jewish welfare recipients—you're just looking after your own kind." This was an issue of social justice. The playing field was not the same.

Paul hit on this kind of racism in an argument with Peter, who started eating only with Jews and ignoring the Gentile believers in their potluck dinners. This racism led Paul to write in Galatians, "There is neither Jew nor Greek, slave nor free, male nor female, for you are all one in Christ Jesus" (Gal. 3:28).

In America, the years of slavery with the ripping apart and destruction of families, Jim Crow laws, lynchings, and economic imbalances have left a painful legacy, the cultural equivalent of an adult who was abused as a child.

It's not as simple as just saying, "Let's forgive and forget and move on now." We can forgive, but racism will still be evident. One interviewee in the book *Divided by Faith* offered John Perkins's analogy of a baseball game that's twenty to nothing in the seventh inning. Then it turns out the winning team has been cheating the whole game. They say, "We're really sorry. Now let's go finish the game." But they're already up twenty points. There is still a legacy. We can have relationship and reconciliation now, but the systemic issues are not really being tackled. It just can't be "I forgive you" and it's over. It's not that simple.

With systemic issues, serving might begin by simply speaking up about social injustices.

I n an interesting passage, Paul compared the church to a marriage. He wrote, "'For this reason a man will leave his father and mother and be united to his wife, and the two will become one flesh.' This is a profound mystery—but I am talking about Christ and the church" (Eph. 5:31–32).

Jesus Christ inside of you and me—the church—is a marriage.

Anita and I were friends before we married, and we work hard at seeing our marriage as a friendship. We try to treat each other like friends. In some ways I can understand that better than the husband-and-wife dynamic. The covenant we made with each other makes us husband and wife, but at a deeper level we are simply friends. Treat your spouse like a friend and watch what can happen.

Very few people see their marriage as having a mission, or purpose. In my mind that's a critical component for success. A mission can be different things, such as providing a loving, empowering context for your kids. For Anita and me the mission is clear: to model, by God's grace, the kind of love Christ has for the church and the church for him. Without a mission, simply fulfilling each other's emotional needs won't be enough. That is too inwardly focused.

I have a very simple equation for success: a healthy relationship plus a purpose equals success. I use it in different areas of my life. With marriage, it goes like this: a healthy relationship plus a purpose equals a successful marriage.

Community is the same way. Some books about community in the church reflect only the relational part. If all we have are internal relationships, we'll become dysfunctionally introverted, or, as my friend Rich Nathan says, just like a box of puppies licking each other. The church must have a mission outside of itself. But if there is nothing but a mission, the infrastructure will eventually collapse into disunity and factions. Both community and mission must be in place.

Developing an outward-focused heart means more than just serving those who are not yet believers. In the move from being inward focused to outward, I think we learn by developing authenticity and vulnerability in a community of believers. *Community* is not just the buzzword in the church today; it's a core value at the heart of God himself—and of course we're to reflect his heart.

In the final chapters of the book of Revelation, John describes a tender scene. By this point in John's narrative vision, we have witnessed a horrifying holocaust followed by global judgment. The story turns a corner when John hears a loud voice cry out, "Now the dwelling of God is with men, and he will live with them. They will be his people, and God himself will be with them and be their God. He will wipe every tear from their eyes" (Rev. 21:3–4). There is a collective sigh of relief, even from the heart of God. Finally.

The longing of God is community with his creation. He wants someone to love and someone to choose to love him. It is the story of the Bible. Community implies with-ness—God is at last with them. The idea of real community is found in who God is. Before the universe came into being, God was community. The power and beauty of the Trinity is revealed in the concept of with-ness. But I believe God describes his heaven as having community with his created beings, who have the power to think outside of his own thoughts and yet choose to be with him.

I can't always hear the voice of God. I struggle with solitude. I am busy by choice. But at times I can hear his voice in my community. I catch glimpses of his grace in my small group when people offer not just advice but their being. I experience God's friendship in my working circle with my pastors. I enjoy my Father with these people. In Larry Crabb's book *The Safest Place on Earth*, he quotes a friend as saying, "I worship so much better when I'm with people I know."[4]

I long for those kinds of shared experiences, perhaps even more so as I grow older.

Did you know there's actually something called Clergy Appreciation Month? Do we really need another card-buying holiday? I'm pretty sure there's a giant conspiracy out there with the greeting-card people. A friend of mine made up a card and sent it to me. The cover read, "When my dog died, you were there. When I lost my job, you were there. When I needed emergency surgery, you were there." Inside it said, "You've been nothing but bad luck."

I think being a clergyman is way down there on the food chain.

How people perceive us has a lot to do with how people receive us. Author Jack Dennison gives a chilling statistic. He writes, "The lion's share of [the churches in America] lack sufficient health to effectively engage the people of their communities. Church growth specialists have placed the percentage of unhealthy congregations at between 70 and 80 [percent]."[5] That means three-quarters of currently existing churches are unhealthy—and therefore dying.

Now add to that the fact that 1,400 pastors quit their jobs each month. Greater Cincinnati is the twenty-third-largest metropolitan area in the United States. There are a lot of spiritually starving folks in that number, people who have never tasted the matchless grace of Jesus.

Cincinnati is a conservative, religious city. But conservatism does not equal spiritual health. And consider this: Greater Cincinnati has about 1.8 million people. The Yellow Pages lists around nine hundred churches. Do the math based on those stats—that's not going to cut it. The root of our racial problems, economic problems, isolationism, alienation, addictions, and consumerism is spiritual in nature. We're trying to fill up the gas tank with the wrong fuel.

I believe we actually need many more churches. Healthy churches with people who are trained to have an outward focus, who believe this is not about them but about others, who know what Jesus meant when he said, "The Son of Man did not come to be served, but to serve" (Matt. 20:28).

When we develop an outward focus to life, everything changes. For instance, Cincinnati has a long history of racial injustice, and in the church at that. In the kingdom of God, African Americans must extend forgiveness to their white brothers. But there's something vitally missing in that for me as a white person. If I don't ask for forgiveness and don't show fruits of repentance by seeking systemic and individual justice, then I'm going to miss the transformational power of love in action. It's always the responsibility of the people of privilege and power to seek reconciliation with marginalized minorities.

Reconciliation, which results from slipping into the skin and understanding the view of those not in power, is what Christianity is all about. Think about it. Paul wrote in his Philippian letter, "Your attitude should be the kind that was shown us by Jesus Christ, who, though he was God, did not demand and cling to his rights as God, but laid aside his mighty power and glory, taking the disguise of a slave and becoming like men" (Phil. 2:5–8 TLB).

Jesus has all the power, privilege, and rights of his Father; they are one. But because of love, he slipped into the skin of a slave. That's why the writer of Hebrews says that Jesus understands every weakness of ours, because he was tempted in every way that we are (Heb. 4:15). He knows what it's like because he became one of us. Only one with power can do that.

Incarnational Christians. That's what each of us is called to be. Slipping into the skin of someone else, to feel what they feel and see what they see and so love them to the fullest. That's the real thing. We do that by listening, by submitting, by loving—and by serving. Paul gives this picture again in 2 Corinthians: "You know how full of love and kindness our Lord Jesus Christ was. Though he was very rich, yet for your sakes he became poor, so that by his poverty he could make you rich" (2 Cor. 8:9 NLT).

God has given the church the ministry of reconciliation. We must use it. It's incarnational Christianity.

A friend sent me an article from the *Dayton Daily News* by outdoor-sports writer Jim Robey. It began with, "People say miracles happen. I'm a believer now, thanks to someone I had never met." Robey had been in line at a Subway restaurant when a mother and her daughter, who were standing in front of him, paid his bill. He was shocked. He stopped briefly at their table on his way out to thank them. He writes:

> "That was kind of you to pay for my lunch, but here, take this," I said, handing them money for the sandwich.
>
> "No," the mother insisted. "It's something I want to do. . . . We go to the Vineyard Church on Indian Ripple Road [and] lately we've been talking in church about doing things for others," the mother explained.
>
> "Well, no stranger ever offered to buy my lunch before. I don't know what to say, other than thank you."
>
> What's shocking is being on the receiving end of generosity. It's miraculous. . . . I can't imagine buying lunch for my hunting and fishing buddies, let alone someone I don't know.
>
> Heretofore, I have proclaimed to my friends that my most valued service to humanity has been to rise early, set forth with rod and gun and bless the waters, the woods and the fields for all. So far, no one has been impressed.
>
> I must find something more. What a better world it would be if everyone expressed kindness to a total stranger. It may not be buying a stranger's lunch, but there are countless other ways. I'm thinking about them. . . .
>
> To our readers who expect information on outdoor topics when they look at this space, excuse the diversion. A miracle could not go unnoticed.[6]

This mom probably had no idea of the effect this would have on some stranger, who just happened to be a sports writer for a newspaper with a daily circulation of over 170,000. She made Christians look a little kinder and a bit more merciful—and church more inviting. It's pretty powerful for a newspaper feature writer to admit to his readership, "I must find something more."

Collection Eight

Small Things

I t was Mother Teresa who said, "We can do no great things, only small things with great love." I think Mother Teresa was a genius. If we're honest, probably very few of us will ever do the big stuff. But maybe in the economy of God, small things carry a lot of weight.

Here's an email from someone who eventually stumbled into our church:

Dear Dave:

After growing up surrounded by hypocritical-Christian examples and attending college philosophy classes, I became an atheist, and the worst kind too. I frequently antagonized Christians, even claiming to be the antichrist just to see them flush.

Years later I moved to Cincinnati. One night, a guy handed me a Starbucks free-coffee card with Vineyard information on it. He walked away without saying a word. Scoffing at the "church gunk" but never turning down free Starbucks, I kept the card.

It was months before I redeemed it. The following morning, I jumped up and went to the 8:30 a.m. Vineyard Celebration. I cannot explain it! I hated mornings more than Christians! I was pleasantly surprised, even for an atheist, to see people who lived what they spoke. The non-pushy environment enticed me to come the next week . . . and the next. I've been coming back for nine years now . . . though I do prefer the 11:30 a.m. service.

Sincerely, Bill

How wacky is that? All it took was a Starbucks card to introduce someone to the body of Christ. And now he has become a dedicated follower of Jesus. We seem to think that nothing counts unless it's the big conversion on the spot, someone falling on their knees in front of us and crying, "Brethren, what must I do to be saved?" That's actually only happened a couple of times in my thirty-something years of following Jesus, and I usually find out that someone had been doing a lot of seed planting and watering way before I got there.

That's okay. I may not be a harvester, but I sure can plant seeds.

Several years ago there was a *New York Times* bestseller called *Don't Sweat the Small Stuff . . . and It's All Small Stuff.* But I'd like to offer a contrarian's view: "Sweat the small stuff. . . . The big stuff is out of your control anyway." I don't think it's the big things in life that turn us inward in unhealthy ways; they have a way of shaking us out of ourselves. It's more the little things that slowly turn us into someone we don't like.

Jesus said, "Whoever can be trusted with very little can also be trusted with much, and whoever is dishonest with very little will also be dishonest with much" (Luke 16:10). In other words, watch the "very little" very closely.

Pay attention to those promptings you get, those intuitive thoughts that pop into your head. If they have the slightest hint of outward focus, they are probably from the Holy Spirit.

Recently I got this great email:

> Yesterday, I felt like I should bring a flower over to my next door neighbor's house and leave it on her front porch where she'd find it when she got home. . . .
>
> I put a yellow rose inside her screen door and wrote her a quick note telling her I was thinking about her and threw in a servant evangelism card from Sunday's program. Of course, the negative thoughts came at me right away. *She'll probably think that was dumb or cheesy or like I'm just trying to drag her to church.*
>
> So, a little while ago, the phone rang and it was my neighbor calling me from work. She thanked me for the rose and said that yellow is her all-time favorite rose color. She then proceeded to say, "Did you know that yesterday was my birthday?" And, of course, I had no idea.
>
> I was totally surprised and overwhelmed. I was so touched because I know God must have wanted to reach her and show his love to her on that day. . . . I felt very privileged to have been a part of the process.

I say, let's get small.

Sometimes when I get bogged down in the complexities of life, I think, *What good is the idea that small things done with great love will change the world?* I have to admit from time to time that I wonder how a "small thing"—a car wash, a bag of groceries, a Coke—is any match for the strategies of the enemy, with his vast malevolent army doing huge damage all over the world.

I visited New York City in the mid-1980s and was surprised at how trashy Times Square was. It felt unsafe, filled with porn shops and people barking at you to come in. Central Park was a drug-infested mess. Crime was through the roof. In the mid-1990s, Mayor Rudolph Giuliani launched a "quality of life" campaign that focused on small things: arresting the people who accosted tourists for spare change and the guys who would spit on your windshield and charge you two dollars to wipe it off. Giuliani's goal was to return civility to the city. Recently in a survey of the twenty-seven largest cities in the United States, New York City was listed as the seventh safest large city, ahead of Denver and San Francisco. Columbus, Ohio, was twenty-fifth. It all began with tackling small things.

Perhaps the small things we do in the name of Jesus have a remarkable impact on the spiritual climate of a city. Zechariah the prophet had a simple encouragement to Judah when they began to rebuild the temple. After years of captivity and the loss of their identity, the people of Judah intuitively knew they would never return to the former glory and magnificence of the kingdom under Solomon. But it was Zechariah who reminded them, "Who despises the day of small things?" (Zech. 4:10).

Let's dream big. Let's make big plans. But let's begin by doing something, no matter how small. Don't belittle the expression of kindness as being no match for the great evil in this big world.

It was the apostle Paul who wrote that it's God's kindness that leads us toward repentance (Rom. 2:4). And that all began with a little Jewish baby born in a backwoods town in the middle of nowhere. That's a small thing when you think about it.

I'm amazed when God takes something really ordinary and does something extraordinary with it. Like with the talking donkey in Balaam's story. Or like turning well water into wine. Or like paying taxes from a fish's mouth. Or like transforming screwed-up people such as you and me into children of God.

Or like using a tiny box of Tide detergent.

We recently had a team of people go to the projects to pass out free small boxes of Tide detergent and some freezer pops for kids. It's very simple: knock on the door and ask whoever opens it if they'd like a free box of detergent. And if there are any kids who come to the door as well—which is normally the case, all of them hanging on to the legs of some mom—offer them a free Popsicle. It's that easy. If you really want to push the envelope (I'm only kidding; this is really simple too), ask them if they'd like prayer for anything going on in their life. How easy is that?

Now get this: that very afternoon a single, unemployed mom was sitting down with her two daughters to count the change in their change jar to see if they had enough money to buy a little box of laundry detergent in the laundry room, because her daughter was too embarrassed to go outside and play in her dirty dress. The doorbell rang, and there were two people with some freezer pops . . . and a box of Tide. The mom began crying as one of the girls took the stuff.

After the people left, the mom asked her thirteen-year-old, "What do you think this means?" to which the daughter replied, "I think it means we need to go to church." The very next day she called the number on the connect card and asked, "What kind of church are you?" She was told about MercyWorks, a Vineyard ministry to the underresourced and marginalized. They walked in that same day and found help with a job, clothing, a little food, and prayer . . . and then told us about their conversation.

It all began with a little box of Tide.

Maybe that's not as cool as a talking donkey, but it spoke volumes to that mom.

I really don't have a big goal in life. I know I'm supposed to—that's what all the books say and that's what the movers and shakers tell me. It's not that I don't have a goal; it's just that I don't think I have a *big* goal. My goal in life is to learn how to be a servant. And once I master that (you can see something screwy right there—I want to master servanthood), my next goal is to help other believers to become servants. I've said before that it's the small things we should be concerned with, not the big things. The big things are usually out of our control anyway. But the small things—like tiny rudders on a big ship—are the things that set the course of our lives.

I recently came across a good passage from the book *The Rest of God* by Mark Buchanan:

> I used to think the spiritual life was mostly about finding and using our gifts for God's glory—my utmost for his highest. More and more, I think it is not this, not first, not most. At root, the spiritual life consists in choosing the way of littleness. I become less so that Jesus might become greater. Its essence is No—No to ourselves, our impulses and cravings, our acts of self-promotion and self-vindication, our use of power for its own sake. It calls us to deny ourselves possessions, rights, conquests that we're tempted to claim just because we can. It is growing, day by day, into the same attitude that Christ had, and by exactly the same means: emptying ourselves, giving ourselves. It is refusing to grasp what we think is owed us and embracing instead what we think is beneath us.[1]

I like that: "choosing the way of littleness." John the Baptist recognized that the most powerful thing he could do when Jesus was on the scene was become smaller, so that all attention went to Jesus: "He must increase, but I must decrease" (John 3:30 NASB).

S erving people can be the easiest thing to launch. If you want to get started and have more fun than should be legal, try this: our patented "Seven Irrefutable Steps to Get Your Highly Effective Church Thinking Outwardly in Autumn." And you might be able to do this without a committee.

Step 1: Go to Wal-Mart.

Step 2: Smile at the senior citizen with the blue vest who has been hired to greet you. Ask him where the rakes are. Tell him, "Thanks so much. And by the way, God loves you."

Step 3: Buy five rakes and one box of big trash bags.

Step 4: Call up four of your friends and invite them to a leaf-raking party at your house on Saturday.

Step 5: Pile in a car on Saturday and go to a neighborhood with a lot of trees. (Don't come to my neighborhood. I live in the suburbs, where they cut down the trees and name the streets after them. I have a stick in the front yard. When the leaf falls, I put it in a sandwich bag and set it on the curb.)

Step 6: Park your car and walk up to a house. Knock on the door and say, "We're from XYZ Church, and we're raking front yards for free. No kidding. Free. Absolutely no donations. Where would you like your leaf bags put?"

Step 7: After raking for an hour, grab a fast-food lunch and debrief. One hour of raking is just enough time to keep it fun for everyone—and long enough to touch four or five families.

That's all there is to it. You might really be surprised at how thrilled some folks are. And you may get some great stories: people who've been through a tough time and haven't had time to rake. Or a recently divorced single mom who's overwhelmed. Or an older couple who have to hire someone to rake.

We had a small group do this outreach recently, and they had a blast. They were turned down only once by a smiling woman who said, "No thanks. I just bought my husband a leaf blower."

This outward-focused act every autumn will not cost you another penny for years. You've got the goods now.

Okay, true pastoral confession time here. In my down times, sometimes I wonder if the small things we do with love really change the world. Sometimes I wonder if the little acts of serving people in practical ways really make a difference. Sometimes I just get tired of this serving stuff and not seeing any big return. It's easy to tell these stories of having an incredible encounter with someone who wants to know more about God only because you washed their car for free, but what you don't hear are the fifty other times when someone just took the free bottle of water and walked away. Are we actually making a difference?

I remember a pastor once telling me that they tried this servant evangelism stuff—this outward-focused thing—and it didn't work. I thought, *That's like saying, "We tried this 'loving people' stuff and it didn't work."* How does serving people with no strings attached not work? If he thought doing that would increase his church attendance, then he's right; it doesn't work. Because there's a string attached. Servant evangelism isn't about growing a big church; it's just about serving people—especially those who don't yet know Jesus—in some small practical way. Period. What's the worst that can happen when you offer someone a free bottle of water? They only like tea? I can live with that. I'm not tapping into any major fear of rejection. But if there is grace present, a divine appointment is possible. Or, to put it another way, if God doesn't show up here, there's nothing we can do.

And so in those times of doubt or fatigue, remember one of my favorite verses: "Don't get tired of helping others. You will be rewarded when the time is right, if you don't give up" (Gal. 6:9 CEV). It's not that you have to crank up any deep stoicism. Just don't quit.

Don't say, "Nothing's happening." For one thing, serving others conforms you to the image of Jesus. That's not bad in itself.

Sometimes people want to know if anything has ever gone wrong in serving people. After over twenty years of doing this stuff, not much has. Years ago a group of people washing windshields for free in a parking lot didn't notice a very large dog in the backseat of one car. As they started on the windshield, the dog had a fit and chewed up the car seats. We waited for the owner to return and of course paid for the repairs. I think that was the worst thing that happened.

Not long ago I was passing out free newspapers on a busy street whenever the traffic light turned red. But one car slowed down while the light was green, and traffic started to back up. That's not cool. The guy in the passenger seat was elderly, had an oxygen tube in his nose, and was moving really slow. He was barely getting his hand up to reach for a newspaper, so I thought I'd help him out by tossing the paper through the open window. Well, it knocked his coffee over on his lap and he screamed. The driver floored it, and as they sped away I yelled, "God bless you! We're from Landmark Baptist Church. . . ."

The pastor of Landmark Baptist, Matt Holman, is a friend of mine. Er, maybe *was* after this.

I recently read a news story of a church youth group claiming responsibility for a bomb scare that emptied out the city hall in Athens, Georgia. Apparently, they left a box of candy for someone to find in a cannon on the city hall lawn. The only problem was that the bomb squad was the one to find it. After evacuating city hall, they used a robot to remove the package from the cannon, then blew up the package with a shotgun, scattering taffy and Jolly Ranchers everywhere.

The youth director told the press, "We take full responsibility for this." I hope she still has her job. I'd certainly hire her!

People are usually genuinely surprised that anyone would serve them for free. They are suspicious, but that seems to make it more fun. When I was passing out the free newspapers, one guy rolled his window down and said, "Is that today's paper?"

That's pretty funny. Did he really think we'd pass out yesterday's paper? I felt like saying, "No, it's tomorrow's. We're a prophetic church."

Instead, I assured him it was. He took it, looked at me like I was from a parallel universe, then smiled and said, "Cool!" and drove off. How fun is that? Later that day I prayed for him, that God would engage him and stir up some questions in his heart about the meaning of life and the need for Jesus.

This is evangelism for people who aren't salespeople. Any of us can do this. Give it a shot.

Just not in a cannon.

R ecently I reread a great passage from Richard Foster's classic
book *Celebration of Discipline*:

> There is the service of small things. Like Dorcas [in Acts 9:39],
> we find ways to make "coats and garments for the widows." The
> following is a true story. During the frantic final throes of writing
> my doctoral dissertation I received a phone call from a friend. His
> wife had taken the car and he wondered if I could take him on a
> number of errands. Trapped, I consented, inwardly cursing my
> luck. As I ran out the door, I grabbed Bonhoeffer's *Life Together*,
> thinking that I might have an opportunity to read in it. Through
> each errand I inwardly fretted and fumed at the loss of precious
> time. Finally, at a supermarket, the final stop, I waved my friend
> on, saying I would wait in the car. I picked up my book, opened it
> to the marker, and read these words: "The second service that one
> should perform for another in a Christian community is that of ac-
> tive helpfulness. This means, initially, simple assistance in trifling,
> external matters. There is a multitude of these things wherever
> people live together. Nobody is too good for the meanest service.
> One who worries about the loss of time that such petty, outward
> acts of helpfulness entail is usually taking the importance of his
> own career too solemnly." . . .
>
> The great virtues are a rare occurrence; the ministry of small
> things is a daily service. Large tasks require great sacrifice for a
> moment; small things require constant sacrifice. "The small oc-
> casions . . . return every moment."[2]

Sometimes loving the people who are closest to us is the most
difficult thing to do. The people who know us best sometimes get
the short end of the stick in terms of our expression of love. Maybe
it's not that we take them for granted; maybe it's because, as Foster
writes, "the ministry of small things is a daily service."

If that's true, then when Paul writes, "Let us not become weary
in doing good" (Gal. 6:9), he gives us a little encouragement to
not get tired in the "small things" department.

A few years ago we met a couple named Andy and Kate who live in Kidderminster, England. They had come to the Vineyard to take part in our SOS—Summer of Service—just to see what it was. It's geared to high school kids and includes five days of worship, teaching, and serving people. Andy and Kate found out about it on our website and flew over here to take part in it. They got hooked on being outward focused and began serving others who didn't yet know Jesus back in England.

While at SOS, they met some teenagers from Grand Rapids, Michigan, who struck up a friendship with them via email. Not long afterward they received an email from a teenage friend across the pond.

> We had SO much fun today! Our family decided to go to the new park in town, Millennium Park, to go swimming and hand out free water bottles. The park is big. . . . It is centered around a really nice man-made lake, and there were HUNDREDS of people there today! Unfortunately we were only able to hand out about seventy or eighty bottles of water, as we only had two medium-sized coolers of water. It was absolutely amazing how quickly we were able to hand out the water, though! It only took my dad, Anna, and me about three minutes per cooler! It was a really fun way to do a water giveaway, because we went swimming between handing out coolers of water so we were able to keep cool! I think if it works out we're going to go there every Sunday after church and hand out water. We're going to invite more people to come along with us and hopefully be better prepared with more water!

Andy wrote in his blog, "It just goes to show that reaching out to people with God's love doesn't have to be a chore, it doesn't have to be all 'religious,' and you can even build it into a family day out. Just think—six minutes of high-octane giving away, and eighty people received a touch of God's love. Now that's what we call a good use of six minutes!"

Who said the English are reserved? This isn't rocket science. It's just a little redemptive kindness.

Have you noticed that the people closest to you are the hardest ones to serve? Maybe you know them so well that all their quirks and idiosyncrasies are hard to overlook. Or maybe, more truthfully, you know they know yours. Or maybe it's just easy to take those around you for granted. When my teenage girls fought with each other, I would tell them, "You wouldn't treat your friends at school like that. How can you treat each other that way? Just pretend like you're friends on a very long sleepover." Of course, they would roll their eyes and fear a mini-sermon was coming, and that was a fate worse than discipline.

I've discovered a simple way to serve those who are closest to you. And if you're a guy and married, this is one of the best things you can do: try listening.

Listening is a powerful act of servanthood and desperately needed in our culture. Turn off the TV. Peel your fingers off the remote. Look the person in the eye. Don't let your mind wander. But just try some active, focused listening. For those close to you, this has high impact. I would even encourage you to name a time where you'll purposefully sit down and just listen to someone in your inner circle—a spouse, a parent, a kid, a friend. Put that time in your Pilot.

If you really want to push the envelope, tell your partner that you are going to spend twenty minutes just listening, with little or no interruption. At key points give them some verbal feedback that you are actively listening. Reflect back to them—"What I hear you saying is . . ."—and then tell them what you heard and ask for clarification. Don't judge. Don't interrupt. Don't glaze over. Just listen. And listen for the sheer purpose of slipping into their shoes and seeing life the way they see it. That's incarnational Christianity.

I think that's the spirit behind Paul's words in Galatians 6:2: "Share each other's troubles and problems, and in this way obey the law of Christ" (NLT). For most of us, not being understood or acknowledged is hell on earth.

Recently we had a team go to a lower-income apartment complex and hand out donated bread. They simply went door to door, offering free bread and prayer.

Two guys on the team walked up to one apartment door and could hear a heated argument. They took the risk of interrupting and cautiously knocked on the door. A man opened the door and our guy said, "Hey, we wanted to see if you could use this bread, but mostly we just came to let you know how much God loves you." The man stood there, stupefied. Then his wife came to the door. The man said, "What did you say?"

"We just wanted to let you know how much God really loves you."

The man stared at them and said, "That's what I thought you said. I can't believe this. We just buried our three-week-old son yesterday. What are you doing here?" Our friend repeated himself and asked if the couple would like to have someone to talk to or pray for them. The team was invited inside and heard more about the couple's story and their overwhelming grief, and then simply prayed for them.

But that's not even the best part of the story. On the way out, after the apartment door closed, they heard the husband say, "See, honey, I told you God cares. We thought he wasn't paying any attention to us, but he just sent them to make sure we knew." That's what the couple had been fighting about.

The kingdom of God came to them in the form of two regular guys with a few loaves of donated bread, and it multiplied. Jesus described it like this: "God's kingdom is like seed thrown on a field by a man who then goes to bed and forgets about it. The seed sprouts and grows—he has no idea how it happens. The earth does it all without his help: first a green stem of grass, then a bud, then the ripened grain. When the grain is fully formed, he reaps—harvest time!" (Mark 4:26–29 Message).

Two guys and some bread from a warehouse club. That's all.

The Effects of Serving on the Servant

T he letter started with, "Dear Dave, I know this isn't how most life-changing stories start, but I experienced God while I was getting a haircut." I was hooked. The writer went on to say:

I had dropped in at Great Clips for a trim. As I waited for an open chair, a guy in hospital scrubs came in, looking tired and speaking all sorts of medical terminology into his cell phone. Always a champion of the obvious, I asked if he was a doctor. He explained that he was a surgeon who had just ended a marathon shift and that he had come in for a haircut before heading home. My name was called, and I headed to my chair.

In the middle of getting my hair trimmed, I felt compelled to pay for the guy's haircut. I'm not a terribly generous person, so I was a little surprised to feel that way. Nevertheless, I paid for his haircut without him knowing it and left. The last thing I ever saw of the doctor, whom I have nicknamed "Surgeon Jeff" because I never learned his real name, was the back of his neck as his stylist trimmed his sideburns.

I don't know what happened to Surgeon Jeff . . . but I know what happened to me. I couldn't stop smiling for the rest of the day. In fact, I even went to bed happy, and when I woke up, I thought about Jeff. For once, I didn't wake up thinking about myself. . . . I didn't think about how much I had to do that day, or why my throat hurt from sleeping with the fan on, or how I want to sleep more than I want to go to work. For once, I thought about somebody else. . . . I thought about Jeff. I thought about what his life was like and whether this small act of kindness made it easier. I wondered if he learned anything about God's love, and I delighted in thinking that he may have.

I am just beginning to experience the joy of being outward focused. The truth is, when I'm focusing on somebody else, I don't have the time to think about all the things I worry about all day . . . and that is a huge gift to me.

Find something today you can do anonymously for someone else. Just leave a note to say that God loves them. Don't wait around to see what happens or ask for a response. Just commit one simple act of grace. You'll be surprised what it does. To you.

In a fascinating article from Case Western Reserve University, bioethicist Stephen Post revealed that he has been studying the effects of kindness on human beings for years. He launched an institute sponsored by the Templeton Foundation to research the effects of kindness—of serving—through serious, peer-reviewed studies. The study is groundbreaking in this arena.

Earlier studies have yielded some intriguing stats. In one report, elderly couples who helped others were only about half as likely to die as those who did not during the five-year research project. Likewise, in a study of two thousand Presbyterians, mental health improvements were more connected with giving help than receiving it. My friend Gary Sweeten and his Lifeway Counseling Center in Cincinnati have long believed this. The article in *Case Magazine* cited another study claiming that the risk of depression was reduced in young people who engage in volunteerism.

Professor Post said that we have had decades of negative influential thinkers, from Freud to Sartre. He wrote, "It's difficult to overstate the negative influence of secular existentialism on the culture of the western world for the last sixty years. . . . It's a view of deep pessimism and cynicism."[1] At the extreme was Harvard biologist Edward Wilson, who believed that Mother Teresa worked with India's poor just to advance her reputation. Now that's cynical. I would think there would have been easier ways to get noticed than bathing leprous, dying people.

It's easy to look upon serving others with a jaundiced eye. Some believe these simple, outward-focused acts are just a marketing tool. We've been called "church-light," "the parking meter church," "the Coca-Cola church" . . . or worse.

I hope someday the church will simply be called "friend of sinners." I'd love to be in the company of Jesus; he didn't seem to mind that title.

Abusinessman who goes to our church was in England for his work and had an outward-focused thought in a less-than-ideal setting. But what was most powerful about the email he sent me was the kicker at the end. It made me think about how healing it is to serve others. He wrote:

> On Thanksgiving Day I was leaving London on a train about 8:30 p.m. I was going to Leeds, England, about a 2½-hour ride. Just out of the station we came to an abrupt stop. There had been an accident on the tracks, and we were not going anywhere for at least an hour.
>
> The train was packed, and nearly everyone was groaning. I climbed over the lady next to me and headed to the dining car and bought every bottle of water they had. I can still hear the lady in the dining car say, "Are you quite sure?" in her thick English accent.
>
> Dave, you wouldn't believe it, but no one refused the "free" water. . . . In five minutes I was out of water and climbed over the lady again, only to hear her say, "You could have saved one for me!" I offered to get her something to drink, but she declined. We did have plenty to talk about for the rest of the journey, though.
>
> I know we have our hands full serving Cincinnati, but what a fertile field the rest of the world is also. Dave, after losing my wife back in February, I never thought I could make it through days like Thanksgiving, but look what God did: he gave me one of my best Thanksgivings ever. Sometimes his love humbles me to tears.
>
> Sincerely, Jerry

I was stunned. I thought about Jerry being away from home on a uniquely American holiday, not knowing anyone and losing his wife nine months earlier. And then to write that God "gave me one of my best Thanksgivings ever" simply because he served some people with no strings attached. The healing power of servanthood.

And it made me rethink my problems, that's for sure.

There is an explosion of scientific studies on what makes people happy. *Time* magazine did a cover story on the science of happiness. The article reads:

> At the University of California at Riverside, psychologist Sonja Lyubomirsky is using grant money from the National Institutes of Health to study different kinds of happiness boosters. One is the gratitude journal—a diary in which subjects write down things for which they are thankful. She has found that taking the time to conscientiously count their blessings once a week significantly increased subjects' overall satisfaction with life over a period of six weeks.[2]

The article suggests taking Sunday nights to write down three things for which you are currently thankful: from the mundane, like your flowers blooming, to the magnificent, like your child's first steps. It goes on to say:

> Psychologist Robert Emmons found [that gratitude exercises] improve physical health, raise energy levels and, for patients with neuromuscular disease, relieve pain and fatigue. "The ones who benefited most tended to elaborate more and have a wider span of things they're grateful for," he notes. . . .
>
> Another happiness booster . . . is performing acts of altruism or kindness—visiting a nursing home, helping a friend's child with homework, mowing a neighbor's lawn, writing a letter to a grandparent. Doing five kind acts a week, especially all in a single day, gave a measurable boost. . . .
>
> [Serving people should be] both random (let that harried mom go ahead of you in the checkout line) and systematic (bring Sunday supper to an elderly neighbor). Being kind to others, whether friends or strangers, triggers a cascade of positive effects—it makes you feel generous and capable, gives you a greater sense of connection with others and wins you smiles, approval and reciprocated kindness—all happiness boosters.[3]

Now, if this is done as unto Jesus, it's even more powerful. Think what bringing a smile to God's face must do to our souls.

Have you ever struggled with how unabashedly the Bible talks about future rewards for believers? For us who are attempting to live as outwardly focused as possible, isn't that sort of a conflict of interest?

Some people believe it's not right that God should offer a reward like some carrot on a stick. That seems dishonest. We think we should live outwardly because it's simply the right thing to do, that a reward will cause impure motives. We have to be careful here. As former atheist C. S. Lewis writes in *The Problem of Pain*, "We are afraid that heaven is a bribe. . . . It is not so. Heaven offers nothing that a mercenary soul can desire. It is safe to tell the pure in heart that they shall see God, for only the pure in heart want to. There are rewards that do not [spoil] motives. A man's love for a woman is not mercenary because he wants to marry her. . . . Love, by definition, seeks to enjoy its object."[4]

The truth is that we don't do anything without some intended result or reward. Even Jesus went through the horrors of crucifixion for a reward. God tells us in Isaiah 53:11 that when his servant would see "all that is accomplished by his anguish, he will be satisfied. And because of what he has experienced, my righteous servant will make it possible for many to be counted righteous, for he will bear all their sins" (NLT). There are two things happening simultaneously here. The intended result benefits someone else— us, for instance. We're here because Jesus gave his life for the just punishment of our self-centered nature and all the behaviors that come out of that. Justice was met in his mercy.

But notice what else happened: he, Jesus, would be satisfied by what would be accomplished in his sacrifice, or, as the writer of Hebrews says, he could see joy on the other side of the cross (Heb. 12:2).

To serve others is not some disconnected, random act of altruism. Hopefully, those served might see the body of Christ and God himself differently. And, even more, they might consider reaching out to the greatest of all servants: Jesus.

I've mentioned that some of us struggle with the idea of being rewarded for serving God. The idea of a reward to come is immensely important and rightly affects the human personality. It's rooted in the Christian virtue of hope, and hope is made confident in us because of our faith. The Bible is filled with the idea of future promises, that there is much more to life than this earthly stuff. Rewards are referenced so much in Scripture because God wants it known that he ultimately rewards his kids. We cannot read Scripture and miss that truth.

But why is it important to him that we should know that? Here's a simple idea: being able to reward his people brings God pleasure. I love both of my girls with equal energy. But when one of them makes an attempt to express her love for Jesus in some way that costs her something, it brings me real joy. Again, my love doesn't change for my daughter, but her attempt to be selfless brings me unbelievable happiness. Being able to express that to her fulfills my enjoyment of the moment.

Jesus told a story about a boss who had an employee who doubled the profits of the money the boss had given him to invest. That made the boss so happy that he wanted to reward the employee with a party. The master said, "Well done, my good and faithful servant. You have been faithful in handling this small amount, so now I will give you many more responsibilities. Let's celebrate together!" (Matt. 25:21 NLT). The employee made his boss smile!

You know, it's pretty humbling to think we have the power to make God smile. It's clear from Scripture that we have the capacity to please God. That's pretty awesome when we think about it. Perhaps that's why Paul wrote in Ephesians 6:7–8, "Serve wholeheartedly, as if you were serving the Lord, not men, because you know that the Lord will reward everyone for whatever good he does."

Let's cause the God of the universe, the creator of all, the redeemer of mankind, to smile. Let's think outwardly, live selflessly, and serve in a practical way.

Regular exercise has always been a challenge for me. I just don't get excited about exercise. An exercise bike I bought soon became a great place to hang my clothes. My motto is, "No pain . . . no pain." I've come to love the wisdom in Paul's first letter to Timothy: "Bodily exercise profits a little, but godliness is profitable for all things" (1 Tim. 4:8 NKJV). That's one for the little promise book.

But get this: in his book *The Healing Power of Doing Good*, Allan Luks, the executive director of Big Brothers/Big Sisters of New York City, writes about research that shows how doing good makes you feel good physically. Here are some of his findings: When serving someone, many people experience an immediate feel-good sensation, which Luks calls the "helper's high." This is followed by a feeling of calmness, increased self-worth, and relaxation. The greater the frequency of serving, the greater the health benefits. And strangely, helper's high results most from helping people we don't know.

Also, people who regularly serve generally have healthier hearts. Why? Partly because serving does two things—it gets the focus off their own needs and onto the needs of others. When they're doing something to meet someone else's need, this reduces stress and makes them grateful for what they have. Both are very important when it comes to heart health and psychological health.

Amazing. A healthier heart, stress reduction, helper's high, calmness, and relaxation. This should count for about thirty minutes on the treadmill, don't you think? It's a lot less sweaty and a lot more fun.

Try exercising your serving muscles today.

D o you really know who you are? If you have received the gift of life from your Father, the Bible calls you a new creation. A child of God. Called by him. Now sharing his divine nature. More than a conqueror. The righteousness of God. Chosen by him. Set free. Strong in him. Joint heirs with Christ. Accepted in the beloved. Victorious and complete in him. Despite your feelings, despite your circumstances, there is one who fought for you, and he gives you those titles because that's who you really are.

Anything contrary to those titles is a lie, and some power is trying to trick you out of who you really are, because that's a threat to the spiritual Mafia that runs this planet.

Sometimes Christians are like a bull in a bullfight. They keep charging at the red cape. Wrong enemy. If the bull would readjust his target slightly and take out the guy with the tight pants and funny hat, he'd be back in the bull locker room dumping champagne on another bull's horns and then drinking tequila in the stable with some cow babe.

Have you ever wondered why every great movie, every great story, has a villain? It's because a villain is built into the drama of the universe. It's the story of an angel who would be king, who rebels and takes over a planet by deceiving an entire world and telling a different story. Jesus calls him a liar. There were serious physical consequences in the Old Testament for anyone who fooled around with the occult—spiritism, talking to the dead, witchcraft, idol worship—because it perverted the true story, the story of love. It is the lie of a great villain who doesn't want you to hear the truth of God's love.

When you know who you truly are, it liberates you to become, of all things, a servant. What a twist in the tale. What if you had nothing to prove to anyone? You don't have to be a big shot or have all the answers. You don't have to have a little more than the next poor slob. You're not defined by what you have or what you do. God has already told you who you are. That makes it easy to be a servant.

Sometime back, *USA Today* did a cover story on what makes people happy. The psychologists in the study narrowed it down to four basic values. First, the happiest people spend the least time alone—that is, they surround themselves with friends. Second, they immerse themselves in activities that cause them to forget about themselves. Third, they don't care about keeping up with the Joneses. And last, they forgive easily.

I've got an idea that combines almost all of these values. Call up three friends and ask them if they want to have some fun. If you don't have any friends, look around your church and invite three people who look miserable. They shouldn't be too hard to find. If you don't have a church . . . well, that's a problem for another book. You need some Christian friends. But you could ask three lonely co-workers if they want to have some fun.

Next, go to a supermarket or a warehouse club and buy some flowers. Then go to a nursing home and pass out a flower to each person. Spend about an hour just listening and asking questions, and offer to pray for anything they would like prayer for. It's rare you'll get turned down. Sometimes I'll ask people, "If Jesus were standing right here, what's one thing you would ask him for?"

Look at how you match up with what the psychologists have said: first, you were around some people who may very well become friends if they're not already—the folks you invited. Not to mention the people at the nursing home. You're already on the road to happiness.

Second, you've engaged in an activity that caused you to forget about yourself.

Third, you probably didn't care about keeping up with the Joneses since you were being generous. Proverbs 11:25 says that the generous prosper and are satisfied; those who refresh others will themselves be refreshed.

Lastly, about that forgiveness thing: sometimes it just works itself in when we practice self-forgetfulness.

I'm trying. I'm finding it's a little easier to forgive others when I have less of myself to protect.

Conclusion

Stories and small ideas about outward-focused living don't mean a lot if I file them in my brain and never let them move into my heart. Funny thing about the brain—it can store stuff indefinitely without us knowing, or at least without us remembering.

Not long ago I visited the small town along the Ohio River where I grew up. It was startling how a glimpse of a front porch could suddenly boot up a memory file I didn't realize was there: I remembered a friend named Steve, who had a buzz cut and was the only person in the universe besides me who read Magnus, the Robot Fighter comics (way before graphic novels). I had long forgotten his face, the haircut, the comic . . . and the porch. I guess there had been no need to pull the file out until that moment.

Later I walked up the graveyard hill overlooking the town. Memories of my scrappy collie-mutt dog and of playing army with hedge balls and dirt clods suddenly came pouring in. I suppose there wasn't a need for those neurons to fire, but they were still there. Those memories all came back in a flash.

But the heart—well, that's another story. Blood flows in and is pumped out. Similar to inhaling and exhaling, the heart receives and gives. It must, otherwise the life in this shell ends. Maybe that's why mystics tend to talk about the heart more than the brain; it's a better metaphor for the Christian life.

Jesus said, "Out of the overflow of the heart the mouth speaks" (Matt. 12:34). Whatever is in there will come out. There's no storage system as with the brain; it all flows out, as it should.

I suspect I'll spend the rest of my life attempting to live the outward-focused life. Learning to be a servant is quite a process. There is a big part of me that just wants to circle the wagons. Or cocoon. Or whatever word describes inward living. And I'm pretty sure my brain would be happy just storing stuff.

But I want my heart to rule, to receive and give. Because as I periodically remind myself, this life is not about me; it's about God and others.

Enough talk. Now let's make a difference in someone's life today. Let's go serve somebody.

Notes

Introduction

1. "Julian the Apostate," Wikipedia, http://en.wikipedia.org/wiki/julian_the_apostate.

Collection One: On Being a Servant

1. Blaise Pascal, *Pensées*, 1660, Section VI, no. 387.
2. Krishnamurti, "The Dissolution of the Order of the Star," Krishnamurti Information Network, 1980, http://www.kinfonet.org/Biography/dissolution.asp.
3. Henry T. Blackaby and Claude V. King, *Experiencing God* (Nashville: B&H Publishing, 1988), 18.
4. Brennan Manning, *Ruthless Trust* (New York: HarperOne, 2002), 5.
5. C. S. Lewis, *A Grief Observed* (New York: HarperCollins, 1961), 5–6.
6. Jone Johnson Lewis, "Rosa Parks Quotes," About.com: Women's History, 2008, http://womenshistory.about.com/od/quotes/a/rosa_parks.htm.

Collection Two: Availability

1. Martin Luther King Jr., "The Drum Major Instinct" (speech, Ebenezer Baptist Church, Atlanta, GA, February 4, 1968).
2. C. S. Lewis, *Letters to Malcolm: Chiefly on Prayer* (San Diego: Harcourt, 1964), 22.

Collection Three: Generosity

1. Lucian, quoted in Philip Schaff, *History of the Christian Church, AD 1–311* (Oxford: Oxford University Press, 1859).

2. Ronald Reagan, "The Brotherhood of Man" (speech, Westminster College Cold War Memorial, 1990).

3. Aristides, quoted in Thomas Ryan, *Disciplines for Christian Living* (Mahwah, NJ: Paulist Press, 1993).

4. C. S. Lewis, *The Four Loves* (New York: Harcourt, 1971), 169.

5. "Menninger's Long History Began with a Small Idea," September 21, 2007, The Menninger Clinic, http://www.menningerclinic.com/about/early-history.htm.

Collection Four: Attitude

1. Annie Dillard, *Pilgrim at Tinker Creek* (New York: HarperCollins, 1998), 30.

2. Ibid., 31.

3. Bob Greene, *Duty: A Father, His Son, and the Man Who Won the War* (New York: HarperCollins, 2001), 212.

4. Oswald Chambers, *My Utmost for His Highest* (New York: Dodd, Mead and Company, 1935), 262.

5. Mike Yankoski, *Under the Overpass: A Journey of Faith on the Streets of America* (Portland: Multnomah, 2005), 217.

6. Warren G. Bennis and Robert J. Thomas, *Geeks & Geezers: How Era, Values, and Defining Moments Shape Leaders* (Boston: Harvard Business School Press, 2002), 69.

Collection Five: Grace

1. Christine Pohl, quoted in Jeff Bailey, "Welcoming the Stranger," *Cutting Edge*, Winter 2001, 2.

2. C. S. Lewis, *Mere Christianity* (San Francisco: HarperSanFrancisco, 1952), 92–93.

3. Ernest Gordon, *Miracle on the River Kwai* (London: William Collins Sons & Company, 1963), 162–63.

4. www.purposedriven.com.

5. Ibid.

6. Philip Yancey, *What's So Amazing About Grace?* (Grand Rapids: Zondervan, 1997), 31.

7. Ibid., 33.

Collection Seven: The Community of Servants

1. Rick Warren, "What's the Difference Between Managing and Leading?" Rick Warren's Ministry ToolBox, August 3, 2005, http://www.pastors.com/RWMT/?ID=218.

2. John Andrew Holmes, quoted in John Cook, *The Book of Positive Quotations* (Fairview Press, 2007), 100.

3. Peter Senge, Art Kleiner, Charlotte Roberts, Rick Ross, and Bryan Smith, *The Fifth Discipline Fieldbook: Strategies and Tools for Building a Learning Organization* (New York: Doubleday, 1994), 3.

4. Larry Crabb, *The Safest Place on Earth* (Nashville: Nelson, 1999), xiv.

5. Jack Dennison, *City Reaching: On the Road to Community Transformation* (Pasadena, CA: William Carey Library, 1999), 41.

6. Jim Robey, "Token of Kindness at Subway," *Dayton Daily News*, December 25, 2004.

Collection Eight: Small Things

1. Mark Buchanan, *The Rest of God: Restoring Your Soul by Restoring the Sabbath* (Nashville: W Publishing Group, 2006), 101.

2. Richard Foster, *Celebration of Discipline* (San Francisco: Harper & Row, 1978), 117–18.

C ollection Nine: The Effects of Serving on the Servant

1. Stephen Post, quoted in Kristin Ohlson, "It's Good to Be Good," *Case* 16, no. 3.

2. Claudia Wallis, "The New Science of Happiness," *Time*, January 17, 2005, A8.

3. Ibid.

4. C. S. Lewis, *The Problem of Pain* (New York: HarperCollins, 1940), 145.

Dave Workman is senior pastor of Vineyard Community Church in Cincinnati, Ohio, a growing church of over six thousand weekend attendees and over a dozen church plants. Vineyard Community Church has become well known for its outward-focused message and ministries.

While crisscrossing the country playing Christian music in 1984, Dave became involved with Steve Sjogren and Vineyard's church plant of twenty people. A couple years later, Dave stepped into a worship-leading role and helped architect the servant-oriented atmosphere of a very different kind of church, pioneering video production and graphic design in the early nineties. After leading worship for twelve years, Dave moved into a regular teaching role and in 2000 accepted the position of senior pastor. He and his wife, Anita, have been happily married since 1978 and are proud parents of two children, Rachel and Katie.

Dave has spoken on developing outward-focused churches both nationally and internationally. For more information, see www.vineyardcincinnati.com and http://daveworkman.blogspot.com.